THE Gator Queen Liz

COOKBOOK

THE Gator Queen Liz COOKBOOK

ELIZABETH CHOATE

PHOTOGRAPHS BY DENNY CULBERT

GIBBS SMITH
TO ENRICH AND INSPIRE HUMANKIND

19 18 17 16 15   5 4 3 2 1

Text © 2015 by Elizabeth Choate
Photographs © as noted on page 192

Library of Congress Cataloging-in-Publication Data

Choate, Elizabeth.
  The Gator Queen Liz cookbook / Elizabeth Choate ;
photographs by Denny Culbert . — First edition.
    pages cm
  ISBN 978-1-4236-3922-0
1. Cooking, American—Louisiana style. 2. Cooking (Game) I. Title.
  TX715.2.L68C456 2015
  641.59763—dc23
                        2015008009

Published by   1.800.835.4993 orders
Gibbs Smith   www.gibbs-smith.com
P.O. Box 667
Layton, Utah 84041

Cover designed by Steven R. Jerman
Pages designed by Melissa Dymock
Printed and bound in China

Gibbs Smith books are printed on either recycled,
100% post-consumer waste, FSC-certified papers or on
paper produced from sustainable PEFC-certified forest/
controlled wood source. Learn more at www.pefc.org.

CONTENTS

DEDICATED TO MY PARENTS:
C J DUPRE AND ELLA GAUTHREAUX DUPRE.
IN LOVING MEMORY

INTRODUCTION

I grew up in the marshes of southern Louisiana, where my father, C. J. Dupre, taught me to hunt, and my mother, Ella Marie Gauthreaux Dupre, taught me to cook. My father was also an excellent cook. Mama would cook up big meals and invite friends and neighbors over to spend the evening eating and eating, and always laughing. I learned everything I know about cooking from my parents.

I was working as head cook at Too's Seafood and Steakhouse in Pierre Part, Louisiana, making homemade food for an all-you-can-eat buffet, when I met Justin. The first time I saw him, I said, "Ooh, that's a good-looking son-of-a-gun." Justin was building a bridge, and his team would come in every day for the buffet, and let me tell you, bridge-builders can eat!

When we were dating, one of our favorite things to do together was hunt alligators. Even though we grew up two and a half hours away from each other, we were both raised the same way. Our parents taught us to harvest alligator and other game, and we've both been tagging our own 'gators since our early teens. We hunt other game, too, and we fish and gather seafood from the rich waters of the Louisiana Gulf.

We've passed the tradition on to our children, Jessica, Destin, and Daimon. Just like my mama did, I use what we harvest to cook big meals for our family and friends. We love to entertain in our home. And we have high hopes that our children will pass down our Cajun heritage to their children as well.

When The History Channel approached me for the show, they had cameras and wanted to interview me and introduce me to the network; I was nervous and sweatin' the whole time. But then they started to ask about my dad and how he'd taught me to hunt. They asked if I still had his gun, and I showed it to them. With my dad's gun in my hands, I finally felt comfortable. A lot of people in Pecan Island and South Louisiana and across the country harvest their own game. For us and many others, harvesting game isn't a sport; it's a necessity. We take pride in the ability to provide food for our table and also play our part in wildlife management.

I wrote this book to show people a new way to use what they harvest and to share our family's delicious recipes. Some of the recipes have been handed down, a few are Justin's, and some have been adapted for our family. Our food is simple and delicious. We make use of our harvest and love to share the bounty with friends and family. There's always room for more people at our table.

With the Cajun 'trinity' of onions, peppers, and garlic; meat smothered in gravy; and my own special Bayou Seasoning (available at www.gatorqueen. com), you're just about set. I hope you enjoy cooking our Cajun food—it's the real deal!

VENISON AND PORK

VENISON & PORK MEATBALL AND POTATO FRICASSEE

SERVES 6 TO 8 PEOPLE

There's nothing better than fresh deer and hog to make a 50/50 ground meat mixture, especially when it comes to meatballs. This recipe can be used with any type of ground meat and will still be a wonderful dining experience.

FOR ROUX GRAVY

1/4 cup vegetable oil

1 large onion, diced

1 large bell pepper, diced

3 tablespoons minced garlic

6 cups hot water

1/2 cup Savoie's Dark Roux

1 (10-ounce) can Mild Rotel Diced Tomatoes and Green Chilies

1 teaspoon parsley flakes

2 tablespoons Gatorqueen's Bayou seasoning

2 tablespoons ketchup

2 tablespoons Worcestershire sauce

1 teaspoon salt

1/4 teaspoon black pepper

FOR MEATBALLS

2 pounds ground meat (venison and pork mixed 50/50)

2 large eggs, beaten

1 cup Italian-style bread crumbs

2 tablespoons Worcestershire sauce

1 tablespoon prepared mustard

3 teaspoons Gatorqueen's Bayou seasoning

2 teaspoons parsley flakes, divided

1 1/2 cups plus 2 tablespoons vegetable oil

1/4 onion, diced

1/4 bell pepper, diced

1 teaspoon minced garlic

2 large potatoes

To make the sauce, in a large cooking pot, add $^1/_4$ cup vegetable oil, diced onion, diced bell pepper and minced garlic. Brown and stir over medium heat until semi-soft and wilted. Once that is ready, add 6 cups hot water along with the Savoie's Roux, Rotel, parsley flakes, Bayou seasoning, ketchup, Worcestershire sauce, salt, and black pepper. Stir generously for 1 minute. Continue to cook over medium heat for about 1 hour.

To prepare the meatballs, place ground meat into a large bowl and add the eggs, bread crumbs, Worcestershire sauce, mustard, Bayou seasoning, and parsley flakes; mix thoroughly together.

In a large skillet add 2 tablespoons vegetable oil, diced onion, diced bell pepper, minced garlic, and parsley flakes. Cook over medium-to-high heat, stirring often, until soft and wilted. Add cooked vegetables to the ground meat mixture and mix thoroughly. Form meat into about 2-inch diameter balls and place in a separate dish. In the same large skillet over high heat add $1^1/_2$ cups vegetable oil. Once the oil is hot, place meatballs in the skillet and cook until well browned on all sides.

Place browned meatballs into the large cooking pot with the roux gravy and let them cook while you peel and quarter the potatoes. Add your potatoes to the large cooking pot and let them cook for about 15 minutes, or until fork tender.

We like to serve this over rice, with potato salad, small sweet peas, and baked bread rolls.

VENISON AND PORK CHILI

SERVES 8 TO 10

The key to a good chili made from venison and wild hog or domestic, is grinding up your venison and pork and mixing it together (50% venison and 50% pork). Wild hog is my favorite for this dish, but it still comes out delicious with store-bought or domestic pork as well. This chili can be frozen in ziplock bags and reheated.

2 tablespoons virgin olive oil

1 large onion, diced

1 large bell pepper, diced

2 tablespoons minced garlic

1 (10-ounce) can Mild Rotel Diced Tomatoes and Green Chilies

4 pounds ground meat (venison and pork mixed 50/50)

6–8 cups water

2 (12-ounce) cans Bush's Baked Beans (honey flavored)

1 (12-ounce) can tomato sauce

$1/4$ cup chili powder

1 packet Sweet'N Low

1 teaspoon garlic powder

2 tablespoons Worcestershire sauce

2 teaspoons black pepper

2 teaspoons salt

2 tablespoons favorite seasoning (I prefer Tony's Creole Seasoning)

In a large pot, add the olive oil and begin browning down the onions, bell peppers, garlic, and Rotel, stirring repeatedly until the onions become soft. Next add your ground meat and continue to brown down the meat with the rest. Once everything is browned, add the water, beans, tomato sauce and all of the seasonings. Let cook over low heat for approximately 1 hour, stirring occasionally. Once the chili is cooked down to the thickness you like, your chili is done and ready to eat. If it is not as thick as you like it, mix 2 teaspoons cornstarch with $1/8$ cup of water and add to chili; stir until thickened. Chili can be eaten many ways—chili dogs, chili Fritos, etc.

SMOTHERED VENISON

SERVES 5 TO 7

The key to a great-tasting smothered deer is to have the meat from whichever part of the deer you prefer (we prefer using the backstrap) cut into 1-inch cubes. Marinate the deer meat in milk in a bowl in the refrigerator for a day or two before you are ready to cook it. The milk takes out some of the wild taste and helps tenderize the meat. You can also add seasonings or Italian dressing to your marinade.

2 pounds venison cut into 1-inch cubes

1 tablespoon prepared mustard

2 tablespoons Gatorqueen's Bayou Seasoning

2 teaspoons Worcestershire sauce

1/2 teaspoon garlic powder

1/2 teaspoon salt

1/2 teaspoon black pepper

1 1/2 sticks butter

2 large onions, diced

1 large bell pepper, diced

2 tablespoons minced garlic

6 cups water

Remove deer meat from milk marinade (see notes at top) and strain it out well. Place meat into a bowl, and add the mustard, Bayou seasoning, Worcestershire sauce, garlic powder, salt, and black pepper. Stir to completely coat the meat. Now set that aside.

In a large pot, melt the butter and throw in all of the onions, bell peppers, and minced garlic. Stir occasionally, letting the onions stick in order to wilt and caramelize for the gravy. When the onions are soft, empty the entire bowl of meat with its seasonings into the pot. Brown well on all sides. Add the water and bring to a boil over medium heat and let the meat cook for about 1 hour, stirring periodically. As the water boils down, check to see how tender your meat is becoming. If it is not tender enough, add 2 more cups of water and let it cook longer, until the meat is as you like it. Once the meat is tender there shouldn't be much water remaining, just a beautiful brown gravy.

Best served over rice with beans of choice on the side.

VENISON AND PORK STUFFED BELL PEPPERS

SERVES 8

Of course, we love to use deer and wild hog ground up 50/50 to make our ground meat. But any type of ground meat will do. Domestic pork is almost as good. Fresh bell peppers are a must.

10 cups water, divided

1 cup rice

1/4 cup vegetable oil

1 large onion, diced

1/2 bell pepper, diced

2 teaspoons minced garlic

1 pound ground meat

2 teaspoons parsley flakes

1 tablespoon Worcestershire sauce

1 (8-ounce) can cream of mushroom soup

1 (8-ounce) can tomato sauce

2 teaspoons Gatorqueen's Bayou Seasoning

8 large bell peppers, whole

1 (8-ounce) bag shredded cheese of your choice
(I prefer mozzarella and mild cheddar)

Preheat oven to 350 degrees.

Add 8 cups of water into a large pot and bring to a boil for the peppers.

Begin cooking the rice according to package directions.

continued >

Meanwhile, in a large skillet, add vegetable oil, diced onion, diced bell pepper, and garlic and cook on a low heat, stirring often, until vegetables are wilted and soft. Place your ground meat into the skillet with the onions and stir until the meat is browned. Then add the parsley, Worcestershire sauce, cream of mushroom soup, tomato sauce, water, and Bayou seasoning. Stir together well and let cook on low-to-medium heat.

While this is cooking down, cut the tops off the whole bell peppers and remove the ribs and seeds. Place the whole bell peppers into the boiling water and leave until they are slightly wilted. Remove bell peppers from water and let them drain. Once the ground meat is cooked and the gravy starts to thicken, add cooked rice to the ground meat and mix thoroughly. Place the bell peppers in a baking pan. Stuff each whole bell pepper with the ground meat and rice mixture, filling it to the top. Finally, spread shredded cheese across the top of each stuffed pepper. Bake for approximately 20 minutes, or until cheese is melted and peppers are hot.

I like to serve my stuffed peppers with creamed potatoes and whole kernel corn.

VENISON AND PORK MEAT LOAF

SERVES 4 TO 6

We prefer to use our own wild hog and deer ground together 50/50 for this meat loaf, but it can be made out of just about any type of ground meat. the best thing about wild game is that there are no steroids or artificial proteins injected into the meat.

1/2 stick butter

1 medium onion, diced

1/2 bell pepper, diced

1 tablespoon minced garlic

2 green onions, diced

2 pounds ground meat

2 teaspoons parsley flakes

1/2 cup Italian-style bread crumbs

1/2 cup Jack Millers Barbeque Sauce

2 large eggs, beaten

2 tablespoons prepared mustard

3 tablespoons Worcestershire sauce

2 tablespoons Gatorqueen's Bayou Seasoning

1 teaspoon salt

1 (23-ounce) jar Prego Mushroom and Green Pepper Pasta Sauce

Preheat oven to 350 degrees. Prepare a standard loaf pan with nonstick cooking spray.

In a small skillet over medium heat, melt the butter and add the onions, bell peppers, garlic, and green onions. Cook these while stirring often until soft, brown and wilted (be careful not to burn).

Place ground meat in a large bowl along with the parsley flakes, bread crumbs, barbeque sauce, eggs, mustard, Worcestershire sauce, Bayou seasoning, and salt; mix together thoroughly. Mold the meat mixture into the baking pan and bake for 1 1/2 hours.

Pour the pasta sauce on top and bake uncovered for 10 more minutes. Now it's done and ready to enjoy.

Best served with creamed potatoes and sweet peas.

SMOTHERED PORK

SERVES 5 TO 7

We prefer to use the wild hog meat that we catch ourselves, but this recipe is really good with store-bought or domestic pork as well.

2¹/₂ pounds pork meat

2 tablespoons prepared mustard

2 tablespoons Gatorqueen's Bayou seasoning

¹/₂ teaspoon black pepper

1 tablespoon parsley flakes

2 tablespoons Worcestershire sauce

1 stick butter

1 large onion, diced

1 medium bell pepper, diced

2 tablespoons minced garlic

1 (8-ounce) can cream of mushroom soup

3–4 cups water

Cut the pork into small 1-inch cubes and place into a large bowl with the mustard, Bayou seasoning, black pepper, parsley flakes, and Worcestershire sauce and mix together well. Set aside and let meat soak in these ingredients

Melt the butter in a large pot over medium heat. Then add diced onions, bell peppers and minced garlic and stir until soft and wilted to a brown color. Add the meat and cook until browned well. Once browned, add the soup and water and continue to stir occasionally over medium heat for about 1¹/₂ hours, or until your gravy is thick and the meat is tender. Just add more water if the meat needs to be more tender and let it cook until you are satisfied with the tenderness.

Best served with gravy over rice, with your preference of beans and bread.

VENISON OR PORK WRAPS

SERVES 6 TO 8

This recipe can be used with just about any meat, but deer and pork are my favorites. This recipe is also great for a beautiful outdoor cookout; we use an 8-ounce bag of charcoal. Of course, it's always better when you have fresh meat to use, especially meat that you can go and get yourself in the wild. Any meat from the deer or hog will work just fine, but I prefer using the backstrap, located on either side of the backbone.

2 pounds deer or pork backstrap

1 (16-ounce) bottle Italian dressing

2 tablespoons Gatorqueen's Bayou seasoning

2 tablespoons Worcestershire sauce

8 jalapeño peppers

2 (8-ounce) packages cream cheese

2 pounds thick sliced bacon

Soak 8 wooden skewers in water for at least 15 minutes so they won't burn once you put them on the pit.

Cut meat into thin slices—about 3 inches long, $1^1/2$ inches wide and about $1/4$ inch thick.

Add the Italian dressing into a large bowl along with the Bayou seasoning and Worcestershire sauce. Cut jalapeño peppers into thin strips (seeds optional) and add the peppers and meat into the bowl and stir well. Let this marinate for about 1 hour.

On a large cutting board, lay down 1 slice of meat, and place 1 strip of jalapeño, and one slice of cream cheese (about $1^1/2$ inches long and $1/4$ inch thick) in the center of the meat slice. Wrap the meat over the pepper and cheese. Now lay down 1 strip of bacon; place your wrapped meat on one end and roll the bacon around the meat bundle, covering it completely. Repeat this process until all of the meat strips, peppers and cream cheese are used.

Slide wraps onto skewers, leaving a little space between wraps; repeat until all of your skewers are full.

Meanwhile, heat the charcoal in your barbeque pit. Once the charcoal is ready, place wraps on the grill or pit, and let them cook until the bacon is crisp but not burnt. You will need to turn your wraps occasionally to keep them from burning.

Best served with potato salad, baked beans, and garlic bread.

VENISON AND PORKBURGER STEAKS

SERVES 6

With this recipe we like to use deer and wild hog but it can still be done with just about any ground meat. Two pounds of ground meat will make 6 good-sized steaks, so use that to determine how many people you would like to feed. This is also a two-step recipe, so the ingredients below will be separated accordingly.

2 pounds ground meat

1 teaspoon celery salt

2 teaspoons Gatorqueen's Bayou Seasoning

1 teaspoon onion powder

1 teaspoon garlic powder

1 tablespoon Worcestershire sauce

1 large egg, beaten

1/2 cup Italian-style bread crumbs

2 (0.87-ounce) packages McCormick Brown Gravy Mix

2 tablespoons vegetable oil

1 medium onion, cut into thin slices

1 medium bell pepper, cut into thin slices

1 teaspoons minced garlic

2 teaspoons Gatorqueen's Bayou Seasoning

1/2 teaspoon salt

1 pinch black pepper

Place the ground meat into a large bowl. Add the celery salt, Bayou seasoning, onion powder, garlic powder, Worcestershire sauce, egg and bread crumbs; mix thoroughly. Separate the meat mixture into 2 big balls and flatten them on a large dish or baking pan to about 3/4 inch thick. Set aside.

In a medium skillet over low heat, add both packages of gravy mix and water slowly (see instructions on packets for amount); mix well.

In a separate medium skillet add the vegetable oil, sliced onions, sliced bell peppers, and minced garlic. Cook over medium heat until all is soft, wilted, and browned. Place meat patties into the same skillet with the onions and pepper, and fry on both sides until dark brown. Add the gravy to the skillet along with 2 teaspoons Bayou seasoning, salt, and pepper, and cook over medium-to-low heat for about 25 to 30 minutes.

Serve with creamed potatoes, small sweet peas, and baked bread rolls.

DEER AND PORK GROUND MEAT SPAGHETTI

SERVES 12 TO 15

This is definitely a favorite of our children. They will eat this for several days, or until it's all gone. We prefer to use deer and wild hog ground up and mixed 50/50 of each, but this recipe will also work with just about any ground meat you would prefer to use. My family loves the flavor of deer and wild hog.

1 stick butter

1 medium onion, diced

1 medium bell pepper, diced

2 tablespoons minced garlic

1 (10-ounce) can Mild Rotel Diced Tomatoes and Green Chilies

2 pounds ground meat

1 (15-ounce) can cream of mushroom soup

1 (23-ounce) can spaghetti sauce

2 (15-ounce) cans tomato sauce

2 tablespoons Gatorqueen's Bayou seasoning

2 tablespoons parsley flakes

1 tablespoon Worcestershire sauce

1 pinch basil

1 pinch oregano

$1/2$ packet Sweet'N Low

3 cups water

2 (12-ounce) packages spaghetti noodles

In a large pot over medium heat, melt the butter and add the onions, bell peppers, minced garlic, and Rotel; cook down, stirring often, until soft, wilted, and slightly browned. Add the ground meat to the pot and continue to stir until meat is browned. Add the mushroom soup, spaghetti sauce, tomato sauce, Bayou seasoning, parsley flakes, Worcestershire sauce, basil, oregano, Sweet'N Low, and water. Stir this well and then allow it to cook for 45 minutes on a low heat.

Meanwhile, cook the noodles according to package directions, just until soft. Separate the noodles with a long fork while boiling to prevent them from sticking together. Drain the noodles and add to the meat sauce, cook for another 15 to 20 minutes on low-to-medium heat, stirring occasionally. Your spaghetti should end up fairly thick.

We like to serve it with baked garlic bread and creamed-style corn.

DEER AND PORK DIRTY RICE

SERVES 5 TO 7

What I call dirty rice is what a lot of people consider to be rice dressing. But in my dirty rice I like to use my own ground-up deer and wild pork meat mixed 50/50. Any ground meat you prefer should still be a hit with this recipe.

1 stick butter

1 large onion, diced

1 large bell pepper, diced

2 tablespoons minced garlic

2 pounds ground meat

3 green onion tops, diced

1 tablespoon parsley flakes

2 tablespoons Gatorqueen's Bayou seasoning

1 pinch black pepper

1 pinch salt

1 (10-ounce) can cream of mushroom soup

1 (10-ounce) can chicken broth

1 (10-ounce) can beef broth

2 cups water

4 cups cooked rice

In a large pot over medium heat melt the butter and add the onions, bell peppers, and minced garlic. Cook while stirring often until onions and peppers are soft, wilted, and slightly brown. Add ground meat to the pot and continue stirring until ground meat is all browned. Then, add the green onions, parsley flakes, Bayou seasoning, black pepper, and salt; mix well. Add the cream of mushroom soup, chicken broth, beef broth, and water; mix to combine. Now let this cook down for about 40 minutes, stirring occasionally (be sure to leave enough water to add the rice). Finally add your cooked rice and mix well while continuing to cook on a low-to-medium heat. Dirty rice should come out semi-moist and should be ready to serve.

SMOTHERED DEER AND FRESH PORK SAUSAGE

SERVES 5 TO 7

For this dish, we prefer to use our own deer and wild pork sausage, mixed 40% deer and 60% pork, but any fresh pork sausage will work wonderfully. When you don't have much time, this is a quick and easy recipe that will delight the entire family.

1 stick butter

1 large onion, diced

1 large bell pepper, diced

1 tablespoon minced garlic

1 teaspoon garlic salt

1 pinch black pepper

1 pinch cayenne pepper

2 teaspoons Gatorqueen's Bayou seasoning

2 pounds fresh sausage links

3 cups water

4 cups cooked rice

In a large pot, melt the butter and add the onions, bell peppers, garlic, and all the seasonings. Cook over medium heat, while stirring often, until onions, and bell peppers are soft, wilted, and browned. Add your links of sausage to the pot and brown well on all sides, until you can cut the links into individual 1 1/2- to 2-inch pieces. Add the water and let cook on medium heat for about 45 minutes, or until your gravy is thick and dark.

Serve with rice and your choice of beans, and baked cheesy garlic bread.

SMOTHERED POTATOES AND SMOKED PORK SAUSAGE

SERVES 4 TO 6

I prefer to use my own deer and wild hog sausage and smoke it myself, but almost any smoked pork sausages will taste great in this recipe. This is another quick and easy recipe that is always great for the dinner table. This recipe can be served with or without rice and is still a treat. If you want rice, remember to leave your smothered potatoes a little moister than you would without the rice.

1/4 cup vegetable oil

1 medium onion, diced

1/2 bell pepper diced

1 tablespoon minced garlic

1 teaspoon parsley flakes

4 links mild smoked pork sausage, cut into 1/4-inch slices

8 small baking potatoes, peeled and cut

into 1/2-inch-long by 1/4-inch-wide slices

2 cups water

1 teaspoon garlic powder

1 teaspoon Gatorqueen's Bayou seasoning

1 pinch black pepper

1/2 teaspoon salt

2 cups cooked rice, optional

In a medium cooking pot, add vegetable oil along with the onions, bell peppers, minced garlic and parsley flakes. Cook over medium heat until the vegetables are soft, wilted and light brown. Add your sausage slices and continue to stir well; cook for about 5 to 7 more minutes. Add the potatoes and continue cooking them on medium heat while stirring, until potatoes are slightly brown on all sides. Add water, garlic powder, Bayou seasoning, pepper, and salt. Keep the lid on the pot and stir fairly often until you see that the water is mostly gone (or completely gone if no rice is desired). Turn off heat, remove cover, and stir until potatoes are slightly creamy and thick.

Best served over a little rice with fried fish on the side.

PORK JAMBALAYA

SERVES 5 TO 7

This recipe is not difficult, but it takes a little time and much attention. Once you add the rice, you must let it keep cooking and may have to add more rice to get it to the thickness and moistness that you desire. Once again, I prefer to use wild hog, but store-bought pork will still be very tasty.

2 pounds pork cut into 1-inch cubes

2 tablespoons Gatorqueen's Bayou seasoning

1 tablespoon Worcestershire sauce

1 stick butter

1 large onion, diced

1 large bell pepper, diced

1 tablespoon minced garlic

1 tablespoon parsley flakes

$1/2$ cup diced green onions

1 celery stalk, finely diced

3 cups water

1 (14-ounce) can beef broth

1 (14-ounce) can chicken broth

3 cups cooked rice

Cut pork into small 1 x $1/2$-inch pieces and place into a bowl. Add the Bayou seasoning and Worcestershire sauce, mix well, and set to the side.

In a large pot, melt the butter and add the onions, bell peppers, garlic, parsley, green onions, and celery and cook on a low to medium heat, stirring often until all begins to wilt. Add the seasoned pork to the pot and continue to stir until your meat is browned and vegetables are wilted and golden brown. Add the water, beef broth, and chicken broth to the pot, cooking over medium heat and stirring occasionally for about $1^1/2$ hours. Be sure not to cook out all of your gravy before adding the rice.

Finally, add about 3 cups of cooked rice to the pot and continue to stir on low heat until the rice has absorbed most of the gravy. It should end up fairly thick but still very moist. Best served with white beans (page 152).

FRIED PORK CHOPS

SERVES 6

3 cups vegetable oil

3 cups all-purpose flour

2 large eggs, beaten

1 (12-ounce) can evaporated milk

1 tablespoon Gatorqueen's Bayou seasoning

2 tablespoons prepared mustard

1 teaspoon Worcestershire sauce

1 teaspoon Louisiana hot sauce

1 teaspoon parsley flakes

6 (1-inch thick) center-cut pork chops

In a large skillet, add the vegetable oil and put aside.

In a large bowl, add the flour and put aside.

In a separate large bowl, add the eggs, milk, Bayou seasoning, mustard, Worcestershire sauce, hot sauce, and parsley, and mix together well.

Place the pork chops into the egg mixture, covering completely, and let sit for about 30 minutes.

When 30 minutes is nearly up, heat vegetable oil in the skillet to 375 degrees. Remove pork chops from egg mixture one at a time and dip into the flour until well coated. Two or three at a time, place coated pork chops into the heated oil and cook until both sides are golden brown. Remove from oil and place cooked pork chops on paper towels in a large pan or dish. Repeat until all the pork chops are cooked.

Best served with creamed potatoes and small sweet peas.

SEAFOOD

FRIED SHRIMP

SERVES 4 TO 6

This is one of my favorite meals, and it's easy to prepare. Of course, the best shrimp to use for this is fresh Gulf shrimp, preferably 21–25 count (shrimp per pound). But medium shrimp still turns out great with this recipe.

2 teaspoons Gatorqueen's Bayou Seasoning

1 teaspoon garlic powder

2 large eggs

1 teaspoon Worcestershire sauce

1 (10-ounce) can evaporated milk

2 teaspoons prepared mustard

2 pounds large shrimp, peeled and
butterflied (cut in half lengthwise)

3 cups all-purpose flour

1 tablespoon baking powder (added to flour)

3 cups vegetable oil

In a large bowl, mix the Bayou seasoning, garlic powder, eggs, Worcestershire sauce, evaporated milk, and mustard; mix well. Add your shrimp to this mixture and mix well until shrimp are completely covered. Place the bowl into the refrigerator for the shrimp to tenderize.

In a separate large bowl, mix the flour and baking powder. In a large skillet, heat the vegetable oil on medium-to-high heat (best not to exceed 375 degrees). Mix shrimp into the flour 10 or 15 at a time, and be sure that each entire shrimp is completely covered with flour. Once the oil is hot, add your shrimp to the skillet and fry for about 4 minutes on each side, until golden brown. After the first batch is done, drain on paper towels and repeat the process of battering and frying until all the shrimp are done. Best served with fried potatoes and a green salad. They also make for a great sandwich or poorboy.

SHRIMP SALAD

SERVES 5 TO 7

We catch our own shrimp straight out of the Gulf of Mexico and there's no better shrimp that I've ever tasted. The fresher the better. For this recipe, I prefer to use the smaller shrimp since I'm blending them anyway, and save my larger shrimp for other recipes. But any size shrimp will do just fine for this easy meal. For this recipe you will need a food processor or blender.

3 cups water

2 pounds raw shrimp, peeled

1/4 cup diced onion

1/4 cup diced bell peppers

1/4 cup minced garlic

1/4 cup diced green onion tops

1/2 teaspoon parsley flakes

1 tablespoon Gatorqueen's Bayou Seasoning

1/2 teaspoon salt

1/2 teaspoon celery salt

8 boiled eggs, peeled

1 teaspoon prepared mustard

2 cups mayonnaise

In a medium pot, add the water, cover with a lid, and bring to a boil over high heat. Add shrimp to water and bring back to a boil. Cook shrimp for 5 minutes, remove from heat and then pour into a strainer. Cool them down with cold water.

Add the onions, bell peppers, garlic, and green onions into the bowl of your food processor or blender and blend thoroughly until very finely minced. Remove minced vegetables from the food processor and place into a medium to large bowl; add the parsley, Bayou seasoning, salt, and celery salt.

Place your shrimp into food processor and blend until finely minced, then add to the minced vegetables and shrimp. Chop the boiled eggs in the processor and add them to the bowl as well. Stir in the mustard and mayonnaise, mixing thoroughly.

Best served on sliced bread like a sandwich or with crackers.

SHRIMP RICE

SERVES 5 TO 7

For this recipe I like to use small or medium brown shrimp straight out of the Gulf. It always tastes better with fresh shrimp.

2 pounds shrimp, peeled

1 stick butter

1 large onion, diced

1 large bell pepper, diced

2 tablespoons minced garlic

2 tablespoons parsley flakes

1 teaspoon garlic sauce

2 teaspoons Worcestershire sauce

2 tablespoons Gatorqueen's Bayou Seasoning

$1/2$ teaspoon salt

2 (10-ounce) cans cream of mushroom or celery soup

2 cups water

4 cups cooked rice

Place your shrimp in a bowl and put them to the side. In a large pot on medium heat, melt the butter and add the onions, bell peppers, and garlic; cook, stirring often, until soft, wilted, and golden brown.

Add parsley flakes, garlic sauce, Worcestershire sauce, Bayou seasoning, and salt to the shrimp; mix together and set aside.

Add the soup and water to the onion mixture and let that cook for about 30 minutes, stirring occasionally. Then add the shrimp with all contents of the bowl to your pot and let that cook for another 10 minutes, or until you still have enough sauce to mix the rice in. Add the rice and mix thoroughly.

Best served with your choice of beans and baked bread rolls.

SMOTHERED SHRIMP

SERVES 6

This is one of our family's favorite meals. There is nothing like fresh shrimp right out of the water here on Pecan Island. And it's so easy to make. When you work all day and you want an easy meal, this is it.

2 pounds small Gulf shrimp, peeled

2 tablespoons parsley flakes

1 teaspoon prepared mustard

1 teaspoon Worcestershire sauce

2 tablespoons Gatorqueen's Bayou Seasoning

1 stick butter

1 medium onion, diced

1 medium bell pepper, diced

2 tablespoons minced garlic

3 tablespoons ketchup

1 (10-ounce) can cream of mushroom soup

3 cups water

4 cups cooked medium-grain rice

In a medium bowl, add your shrimp, parsley, mustard, Worcestershire sauce, and Bayou seasoning; mix well and set aside.

In a large pot melt the butter and add the onions, peppers, and garlic. Let this cook down for 15–20 minutes, until onions are browned, letting them stick a little and then stir. Once the vegetables have browned, add the ketchup, soup, and water; mix well and let this cook for 20 minutes. Then add the seasoned shrimp, stirring well. Cook this down for 20 minutes, until thick.

Serve over rice. Goes well with green bean casserole (page 146).

SHRIMP FRICASSEE

SERVES 8 TO 10

1 cup vegetable oil

1 cup all-purpose flour

1 large onion, diced

1 large bell pepper, diced

2 tablespoons minced garlic

$1/2$ cup chopped green onions

1 (10-ounce) can Mild Rotel Diced
Tomatoes and Green Chilies

6 cups water

$1/2$ cup parsley flakes

1 (8-ounce) can tomato sauce

$1/2$ rib celery, chopped

1 teaspoon Louisiana Hot Sauce

2 tablespoons Gatorqueen's Bayou Seasoning

1 teaspoon salt

1 teaspoon black pepper

1 (10-ounce) can cream of mushroom soup

2 pounds white Gulf medium shrimp, peeled

4 cups cooked rice

In a large pot over low heat, add the vegetable oil and flour. Stir together to make a roux and cook until flour starts to brown. Once the roux is brown, add the onions, peppers, garlic, green onions, and Rotel, stirring often until vegetables have wilted down. Stir in the water and add the parsley flakes, tomato sauce, celery, seasonings, and soup. Cook this over medium heat for 1 hour and 15 minutes; stirring occasionally. Add the shrimp and cook for another 10 minutes, until your stew is thick and full of flavor. Season to taste.

Serve over rice with potato salad and white beans.

STUFFED SHRIMP

SERVES 4 TO 8

Depending on how many shrimp your family can eat, that's how many you fry. The rest of your stuffed shrimp, place into a pan, cover them and put in your freezer until you are ready to defrost and fry again. My family and I eat 3 stuffed shrimp each, so 12 stuffed shrimp for 4 people.

2 pounds large Gulf shrimp (21–25 count), peeled and deveined, tails on

1 large onion, diced

1 medium bell pepper, diced

3 green onions, diced

3 tablespoons minced garlic

1 stalk celery, diced

1 stick butter

2 pounds dark claw crabmeat

1 cup water

2 tablespoons Gatorqueen's Bayou Seasoning

1 teaspoon salt

$1/2$ teaspoon black pepper

2 eggs, beaten

2 cups Italian bread crumbs

3 cups all-purpose flour

6 cups vegetable oil, for deep-frying

Place your shrimp into a bowl. Place the onions, bell peppers, green onions, garlic, and celery into the bowl of a food processor and process to a tiny mince. In a large skillet, melt the butter and add the onion mixture; cook this down for 20 minutes over low heat. Add your crabmeat and water and let this cook down until water is gone and mixture is thick. Remove from heat and let this cool down for 10–15 minutes. Then pour mixture into a large bowl. Add the seasoning, eggs, and bread crumbs and mix until well combined and thick.

Take the shrimp one at a time and wrap completely with the crabmeat mixture at least $1/2$ inch thick. Place the flour into a bowl, toss the covered shrimp in flour until completely covered, shake off excess flour, and place shrimp to the side. Repeat until all the shrimp are ready.

Heat the oil in a large, deep pot until good and hot. Fry shrimp until golden brown, flipping often, and place on paper towels to drain.

Serve with Cajun Dip (page 147).

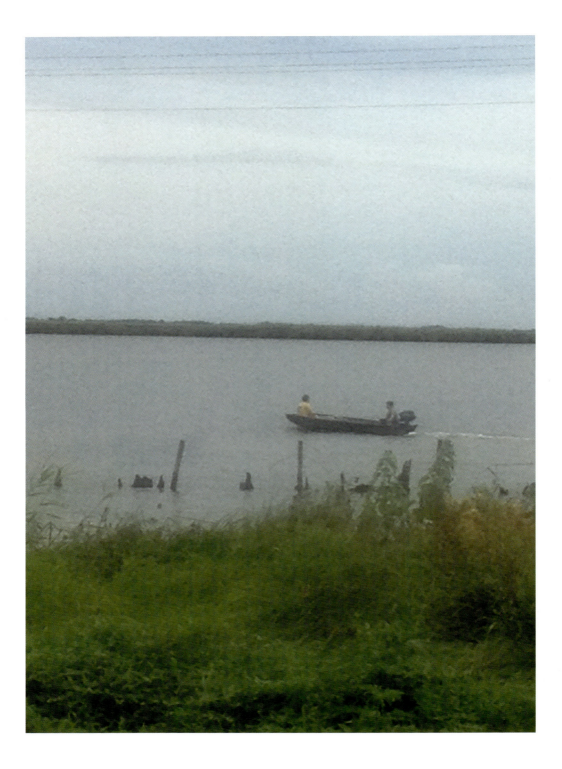

SHRIMP BOIL

SERVES 10 TO 12

A shrimp boil is an occasion to invite people over. Everybody digs in for a good meal and a great time. If you're expecting a larger crowd, just add more shrimp and vegetables to the pots.

FOR THE VEGETABLES
10 small red potatoes

6 small corn on the cob

4 large onions, quartered

4 quarts water

$1/2$ cup powdered crab boil (such as Zatarain's)

$1/4$ cup salt

FOR THE SHRIMP
4 quarts water

$1/3$ cup salt

$1/2$ cup powdered crab boil

1 tablespoon vegetable oil

4 pounds white Gulf shrimp (21–25 count)

You need 2 large pots. In one large pot add potatoes, corn, onions, 4 quarts water, $1/2$ cup crab boil and $1/4$ cup salt. Bring this to a hard boil for 20–25 minutes, or until the potatoes are tender. Remove from heat, drain water and place to the side; cover to keep warm.

In a second large pot add 4 quarts of water, $1/3$ cup salt, $1/2$ cup crab boil and oil; bring to a hard boil with the lid on. Once the shrimp water is to a hard boil, drop your shrimp into the water, letting the water come to boil again. Boil for 3 minutes. Turn your fire off, letting shrimp soak for 2–5 minutes. Taste a shrimp to see if it's seasoned enough; if not leave them longer, until it's to your taste but not longer than a couple of minutes. Drain the water.

To serve, spread out some old newspapers on your table and pour the shrimp, potatoes and corn into the center.

SUDDENLY SHRIMP SALAD

SERVES 4 TO 6

Quick and easy meal and tastes good.

1 pound small Gulf shrimp, peeled

2 (7-ounce) boxes Suddenly Pasta
Salad Ranch and Bacon

1 1/2 cups Blue Plate Mayonnaise

1 (8-ounce) bag mild cheddar cheese

1/2 teaspoon Gatorqueen's Bayou Seasoning

In a medium pot, boil your shrimp for 5–10 minutes until pink. Remove from heat, drain water and place shrimp into a bowl to cool.

In a large pot, cook the noodles in the 2 boxes of Suddenly Salad according to package directions. Remove from heat, drain the water and rinse with cold water to stop the cooking. Add the noodles to the shrimp. Add the two packets of ranch mix into your bowl, with the mayonnaise, cheese, and Bayou seasoning. Mix well.

Good chilled or at room temperature.

FISH COUBION

SERVES 5 TO 7

For this recipe my family and I normally prefer to use redfish, garfish, or catfish, but we've also used bass, crappie, and trout. So almost any kind of fish will work as long as it's as fresh as you can get it. It always tastes better when you catch your own.

2 pounds fish filets of choice

1 1/2 tablespoons virgin olive oil

1 large onion, diced

1 large bell pepper, diced

2 teaspoons minced garlic

1/2 teaspoon celery salt

1 (10-ounce) can Mild Rotel Diced
Tomatoes and Green Chilies

2 (10-ounce) cans dark golden cream of mushroom soup

2 tablespoons Gatorqueen's Bayou Seasoning

1/2 teaspoon salt

3 cups water

4 cups cooked rice

Cut fish filets into about 1-inch nuggets and place to the side. In a large pot over medium heat, add the olive oil, onions, bell peppers, garlic, celery salt, and Rotel, and cook, stirring often, until the onions and bell peppers are soft, wilted, and slightly brown. Now you can add the soup, Bayou seasoning, salt and water, and let cook on a medium heat for about 30 minutes, stirring occasionally. Finally, add the fish to the pot and let cook for 15–20 more minutes or longer to make sure the gravy is fairly thick.

Best served over rice with creamed corn and baked bread rolls.

BAKED FISH

SERVES 8 TO 10

In Louisiana we do a lot of fishing down in these parts. My mom and dad raised us on fried catfish and rice and beans. And people from all over the country come to fish in our south Louisiana Sportsman's Paradise. It doesn't matter what type of filets you use, it could be catfish, redfish, red snapper—whatever fish you prefer.

6 (1-pound) fish filets of choice

1 teaspoon minced garlic

3 tablespoons Gatorqueen's Bayou Seasoning

2 tablespoons Worcestershire sauce

1 tablespoon prepared mustard

$1/4$ teaspoon lemon juice

1 tablespoon parsley flakes

2 medium onions, sliced thin

2 medium bell peppers, sliced thin

3 sticks butter, cut into thin slices

Preheat oven to 375 degrees.

Rinse your filets, drain well and place to the side.

In a large bowl put the garlic, Bayou seasoning, Worcestershire sauce, mustard, lemon juice, and parsley flakes; mix well. Add your filets to this mixture, making sure they are well coated. Place filets in a large baking pan and cover with the onion, pepper and butter slices. Pour the remaining seasoning mixture from your bowl over the top and bake for $1^1/2$ hours uncovered. Fish should be tender on the inside and somewhat firm on the outside.

FISH PATTIES (BOULETTES)

SERVES 6 TO 8

Using a food processor to chop the fish and vegetables

2 pounds catfish, cut in to small pieces

1 large onion, chopped

1/2 large bell pepper, chopped

1/2 cup chopped green onions

2 tablespoons minced garlic

2 medium white potatoes, peeled and chopped

1/2 cup peeled and chopped sweet potato or carrots

2 tablespoons parsley flakes

3 large eggs, beaten

2 tablespoons Worcestershire sauce

2 tablespoons prepared mustard

1/4 cup Gatorqueen's Bayou Seasoning

1/2 teaspoon salt

1/2 teaspoon black pepper

1 1/2 cups plain bread crumbs

3 cups vegetable oil for frying

Place the pieces of catfish into the bowl of a food processor and mince well. Move fish to a large bowl.

Place the onions, peppers, green onions, garlic, potatoes, and sweet potato or carrot into your processor and mince well. Add to the fish in your bowl. Add the parsley flakes, eggs, Worcestershire sauce, mustard, Bayou seasoning, salt, pepper, and bread crumbs. Mix all ingredients until well combined.

Put the oil to heat in a skillet. Wet your hands with water and make the patties, about the size of a woman's palm and 1/2 inch thick. Place patties a couple at a time in the hot oil and fry until dark brown; flip, and cook the other side. Let drain on paper towels.

Makes good sandwiches, or serve with rice and white beans.

FRIED FISH

SERVES 5 TO 7

It's always better to have fresh fish filets that you have caught yourself, but there are always places you can buy fresh fish. This recipe works with any kind of fish that we have ever caught, and that's quite a few.

2 pounds fresh fish filets

2 large eggs, beaten

1 tablespoon Gatorqueen's Bayou Seasoning

1 teaspoon salt

1 teaspoon Worcestershire sauce

3 tablespoons prepared mustard

3 cups all-purpose flour

4 cups vegetable oil

Cut filets into long, thin strips about 4–5 inches long and about $1/2$ inch thick and $1/2$ inch wide. In a large bowl, add all of the ingredients except the fish, flour, and oil, and mix all together well. Add your fish to the mixture and mix well again. In a separate bowl or large ziplock bag, add the flour.

In a large skillet, add the vegetable oil and begin heating to approximately 375 degrees. While that's heating up, put about 10 strips of fish into the flour and make sure the fish is covered with the flour. Remove the fish from the flour and place into the hot oil; fry until slightly dark golden brown. Remove from oil and place on paper towels to soak up excess oil. Repeat the process until all of the fish are fried.

Best served with seasoned white beans over rice and fried potatoes.

BOILED BLUE CRABS

SERVES 4 TO 6

When boiling your own crabs, the most important thing to remember is that the crabs should still be alive when you put them into the pot. Otherwise the meat will be soft and have an unpleasant flavor. Live crabs are delicious. This recipe can be used with just about any amount of crabs, just use more or less of the seasonings. We normally use a 48-quart boiling pot with a cooking basket (strainer) that fits into the pot and a high-pressure propane burner connected to a propane bottle. You can also cook them in a smaller pot or even on the stove. Water will always come to a boil quicker if the pot is covered with a lid. Recipe by Justin Choate.

3 dozen blue crabs

1 (26-ounce) round box iodized salt

1 (8-ounce) bottle liquid crab boil

4 tablespoons minced garlic

2 lemons, sliced into thin rounds

1 stick butter

Place your crabs into the basket or strainer and rinse them well. Then place the basket into your pot and fill the pot with water until it almost covers the top of the crabs. Remove the crabs and set aside. Light the burner and set on a high heat to begin boiling the water. After the burner is lit, add all of the ingredients above to the pot, except for the crabs. Once the water comes to a hard boil, place your crabs into the water. At this point the water will stop boiling. Once the water comes to a boil again, let the crabs boil for 10 minutes, then remove them from the pot and place into an ice chest (cooler), or whatever you have available.

Best served with boiled potatoes, boiled corn on the cob, and Cajun Dip (page 147).

CRAB FRICASSEE

SERVES 8 TO 10

1 cup vegetable oil

1 cup all-purpose flour

1 large onion, diced

1 large bell pepper, diced

1 teaspoon minced garlic

$1/3$ cup chopped green onions

1 (10-ounce) can Mild Rotel Diced
Tomatoes and Green Chilies

6 cups water

1 tablespoon ketchup

2 tablespoons Gatorqueen's Bayou Seasoning

1 teaspoon Worcestershire sauce

$1/2$ teaspoon Louisiana Hot Sauce

$1/2$ teaspoon salt

3 pounds lump white crabmeat

In a large pot over medium heat, begin making your roux by adding the oil and flour, stirring constantly, until it is dark brown. Add the onions, peppers, garlic, green onions, and Rotel, stirring constantly. Add water ketchup and seasonings. Stir together until well mixed, and cook for $1 1/2$ hours, to where the water is cooking out and your gravy starts to thicken. Add the crabmeat and cook for 15 more minutes. The longer you cook your gravy, the thicker it will become. Adjust seasonings to taste.

Serve over rice with potato salad on the side.

SHRIMP OR CRAWFISH FETTUCCINE

SERVES 8 TO 10

It always makes a better meal when your food is fresh, that's why I always try to get the freshest Gulf shrimp, or local crawfish (not imported) that I can. It's best to use small or medium brown or white Gulf shrimp. But if you only have large shrimp, dice each shrimp into 2 or 3 pieces.

1 stick butter

1 large onion, diced

1 large bell pepper, diced

1 tablespoon minced garlic

1/4 cup diced jalapeño peppers

1/2 rib celery, diced fine

2 green onions, diced fine

2 tablespoons parsley flakes

2 cups water

1 (10-ounce) can cream
of mushroom soup

2 cups half-and-half

2 (12-ounce) packages fettuccine noodles.

2 pounds small or medium
shrimp or crawfish, peeled

1 tablespoon Gatorqueen's
Bayou Seasoning

2 pounds Velveeta block cheese,
cut into large cubes

In a large cooking pot, melt the butter over low heat. Next, add the onions, bell peppers, minced garlic, jalapeños, celery, green onions, and parsley flakes and cook on low-to-medium heat while stirring often, until vegetables are soft and wilted. Now add 2 cups of water, soup, and half-and-half, and continue to stir and cook on low-to-medium heat.

Meanwhile, cook the noodles according to package directions, using a large fork to separate them and prevent from sticking together. Cook noodles for 18 minutes, then drain and set aside.

To the pot with cream and vegetables, add the shrimp or crawfish and continue stirring on a low-to-medium heat for about 7 minutes. Add the Bayou seasoning and cubes of Velveeta, stirring continuously until all of the cheese is melted. Now add the noodles to the shrimp mixture and cook on low heat, stirring often, for about 15 more minutes.

BOILED CRAWFISH

SERVES 7 TO 10

For this recipe it is important to have live crawfish, preferably Louisiana crawfish. We use a 30- to 48-quart pot with its own basket strainer and a high-pressure propane burner. It is best to have a lid for the pot so that the water comes to a boil faster. This recipe can be used with more or less crawfish than what is shown below, just by adjusting a proportional seasoning amount. One sack of live crawfish normally varies from 28 to 40 pounds, depending on the size of the crawfish. You will also need a 48-quart ice chest. This recipe is from my husband, Justin Choate.

30 pounds live crawfish	3 tablespoons minced garlic
2 (26-ounce) round boxes iodized salt	$1^1/_2$ lemons, sliced into thin rounds
1 (8 ounce) bottle liquid crab boil	1 (16-ounce) bag powdered crab boil
1 stick butter	

Place the crawfish into your ice chest and rinse them thoroughly, removing any that may be dead, then pour them into the basket and place them into the pot. Begin adding water to the pot until the water almost covers the crawfish. Once water is to the right level, remove the basket of crawfish from the pot and place them to the side. Now light your burner and begin heating the water on a high heat.

Add 1 box of salt, the liquid crab boil, butter, garlic, and lemons to the pot. Rinse the ice chest while the water is heating and then add water 5 inches deep into the ice chest along with the 16 ounces of powdered crab boil seasoning and the other box of salt; set aside.

Once the water begins boiling hard, place your basket of crawfish back into the pot and cover. When the water begins to boil hard again, let the crawfish boil for 5 minutes, then remove them from the pot and pour them immediately into the seasoned water in the ice chest. Shake and mix the crawfish in the seasoned water for about 1 minute. Finally, drain the water out of the ice chest and your crawfish should be done. They are easy to peel, with seasoning on the inside and none on the outside. We normally serve this with boiled potatoes, boiled corn on the cob, and Cajun Dip (page 147).

FRIED FROG LEGS

SERVES 4 TO 6

Here in Louisiana, fried frog legs are a delicacy. We enjoy going out in the ditches and swamps at night with our children and catching bullfrogs. Frogs must be skinned before cooking, and normally the back legs are the best, but the entire frog can be fried and is a very tasty meal. Many supermarkets carry frog legs. This recipe requires the frog legs to be double battered, and once done you will see why it's such a delicacy.

30 frog legs	1 teaspoon garlic powder
2 large eggs, beaten	2 tablespoons prepared mustard
1/2 cup half-and-half	1/2 teaspoon hot sauce of your choice
1/2 teaspoon black pepper	1 teaspoon Worcestershire sauce
1 teaspoon salt	Pinch of paprika
1/2 teaspoon celery salt	3 cups flour
2 teaspoons Gatorqueen's Bayou Seasoning	3 cups vegetable oil

To get started, place the frog legs into a large bowl. In a separate large bowl add remaining ingredients except the flour and vegetable oil, and mix them all together thoroughly.

Add the frog legs to the egg mixture, mix well and let frog legs sit in mixture for about 30 minutes.

In another separate large bowl add the flour. Take one frog leg at a time and place into the flour, covering completely. Dip the flour-covered frog leg back into the egg batter, covering it completely once again. Finally, place the leg back into the flour again, covering it well, and then place on a separate dish until you have enough of them to begin frying.

In a large skillet, add vegetable oil and heat it to 375 degrees. Place about 6–10 frog legs at a time into the oil and fry until golden brown (you may have to turn the legs as they fry). Repeat this process until all are cooked.

Best served with fried potatoes and a green salad.

FRIED CRAB CLAWS

SERVES 5 TO 7

In Louisiana we have Blue Crabs. If you can get these, they are awesome. Steam them for 15 minutes in hot water and peel the claws. The crab itself can be used for crab stew.

2 cups vegetable oil

2 large eggs, beaten

1 (12-ounce) can evaporated milk

2 tablespoons Gatorqueen's Bayou Seasoning

1 teaspoon salt

1 teaspoon Louisiana Hot Sauce

2 pounds medium-to-large crab claws

2 cups all-purpose flour

Pour oil into a large skillet and heat on low until your batter is ready.

In a medium bowl, add eggs, milk, seasoning, salt and hot sauce, whisking well. Add the crab claws.

In a separate bowl add the flour. Remove crab claws from the batter and mix these into the flour. Fry coated claws in hot oil until a golden color.

Serve as an appetizer with Cajun Dip (page 147).

CRAWFISH ÉTOUFFÉE

SERVES 5 TO 7

In Louisiana we have a Crawfish season—late February into May, sometimes later. These crawfish are a delicacy for people not only in Louisiana but all over the country.

2 pounds Louisiana crawfish tails

1$1/2$ sticks butter

1 large bell pepper, diced

1 large onion, diced

2 teaspoons minced garlic

3 green onions, chopped

2 tablespoons Gatorqueen's Bayou Seasoning

$1/4$ cup Worcestershire sauce

$1/2$ teaspoon salt

1 teaspoon parsley flakes

1 tablespoon prepared mustard

1 (10-ounce) can cream of mushroom soup

1 (10-ounce) can Mild Rotel Diced
Tomatoes and Green Chilies

3 cups water

Rinse your crawfish tails, place them in a bowl and set aside.

In a large pot melt the butter. Add the peppers, onions, garlic, and green onions. Saute until the vegetables are wilted and slightly brown. Add your crawfish, stirring well for about 5 minutes. Then add the Bayou seasoning, Worcestershire sauce, salt, parsley flakes, mustard, soup, Rotel, and water. Cook on low heat until water has cooked out and gravy is thick, about 20 minutes.

Serve over rice, with a green salad on the side. Or serve over fried fish with cheddar cheese sprinkled on top. Yum, yum!

SHRIMP AU GRATIN

SERVES 6 TO 8

1 stick butter

1 large onion, finely diced

1 large bell pepper, finely diced

1 teaspoon minced garlic

1 rib celery, finely diced

1/2 cup chopped green onions

1/2 teaspoon parsley flakes

2 cups water

2 tablespoons flour

1/2 teaspoon salt

1/2 teaspoon black pepper

1/2 teaspoon celery salt

4 cups half-and-half

1 pound Velveeta cheese cut into cubes

2 pounds shrimp, peeled

In a large pot, melt the butter then add the onions, peppers, garlic, celery, green onions, and parsley. Cook until vegetables are wilted, then add water. Let simmer over low heat for 20 minutes, or until the water is cooked out. Add flour to onions and stir until all the liquid is absorbed. Add the salt, pepper, celery salt, half-and-half, pouring slowly and stirring constantly to fully incorporate into the flour mixture. Add cheese and stir until melted. Add shrimp and cook for 10 minutes. Best served over a filet of fried fish.

FRIED CRAWFISH

SERVES 5 TO 7

1 1/2 cups half-and-half

2 large eggs

1 tablespoon Gatorqueen's Bayou Seasoning

1/4 teaspoon parsley flakes

1 teaspoon Worcestershire sauce

1 teaspoon prepared mustard

2 pounds Louisiana crawfish tails

4 cups all-purpose flour

4 cups vegetable oil

In a medium-sized bowl, pour the half-and-half and crack the eggs. Add Bayou seasoning, parsley, Worcestershire sauce, and mustard and whisk well until everything is incorporated. Add your crawfish tails to batter, and set aside for 30 minutes, letting the crawfish soak up the batter.

Pour the flour into a bowl. Start heating the oil in a large skillet. Remove crawfish tails from batter and pass into the flour, shaking off excess flour. Fry your crawfish until lightly golden color, and put them to drain on paper towels. Best served with potato salad, or just pop them in your mouth.

CRAWFISH ÉTOUFFÉE AND FRIED FISH FILETS

SERVES 8 TO 10

If crawfish have fat on the tails, I normally wash them off, but some people like it. It's all what you prefer.

CRAWFISH

1 large onion

1 medium bell pepper, green or red

2 teaspoons minced garlic

3 stems green onions

1 1/2 sticks butter

1 (10-ounce) can Mild Rotel Diced Tomatoes and Green Chilies

1 (10-ounce) can cream of mushroom soup

1 1/2 cups water

2 pounds crawfish tails

2 tablespoons Gatorqueen's Bayou Seasoning

1/4 cup Worcestershire sauce

2 teaspoons garlic powder

1/2 teaspoon salt

1/2 teaspoon parsley flakes

1 tablespoon prepared mustard

1 teaspoon black pepper

Cut the onion, pepper, garlic, and green onions into small pieces. In a pot, melt the butter on medium heat and add the cut-up vegetables. Stir well and cook until wilted. Stir in Rotel and cream of mushroom. Then add water and cook slowly on medium heat.

In a separate bowl, add your crawfish tails (make sure they are drained of water), Bayou seasoning, Worcestershire, garlic powder, salt, parsley, mustard, and black pepper. Mix these ingredients around to cover all the crawfish tails. Let the tails sit in the bowl. When the water is almost cooked out of the onions, add the tails, stirring all ingredients together. Cook down for 10–15 minutes, until your gravy is thick and tails are cooked and tender. Once your étouffée is cooked, cover and place to the side.

FRIED FISH FILETS

4–6 (8-ounce) catfish filets

3 large eggs

3 tablespoons Gatorqueen's Bayou Seasoning

2 teaspoons garlic powder

1 teaspoon salt

2 teaspoons Worcestershire sauce

$1/2$ cup mustard

3 cups oil

2 cups all-purpose flour

1 (12-ounce) bag shredded mild cheddar cheese

Lay your catfish filets on a cutting board, cut in half and make several knife cuts across top of the fish to enable the fish to cook through. Set aside in a bowl.

In a separate bowl, whisk together eggs, Bayou seasoning, garlic powder, salt, Worcestershire, and mustard. Pour ingredients over the fish, mixing well.

In a frying pan heat 3 cups of oil to 350–375 degrees (do not exceed 375 or it will burn). Mix the fish into the flour, coating them well on each side. Place fish into the oil and fry on each side until dark golden brown. They should be crunchy on the outside and tender on the inside. Once the fish is done, drain on paper towels.

To serve, place one fish filet on a plate, cover the fish with étouffée, and sprinkle cheese on top. Delicious!

CRAB AU GRATIN

SERVES 6 TO 8

1 stick butter

1 large onion, finely diced

1 large bell pepper, finely diced

1 rib celery, finely diced

1 teaspoon minced garlic

$^1/_2$ teaspoon parsley flakes

$^1/_2$ teaspoon salt

$^1/_2$ teaspoon black pepper

$^1/_2$ teaspoon thyme

$^1/_4$ teaspoon basil

2 cups water

2 pounds crabmeat

4 cups half-and-half

1 pound Velveeta cheese, cut into small cubes

2 tablespoons flour

In a large pot, melt the butter, then add the onions, peppers, celery, garlic, parsley, salt, pepper, thyme and basil. Cook and stir until mixture is wilted, then add water. Cook this down for 20 minutes on a low heat. Once the water is gone and the onions are cooked down, add your crabmeat and sauté for 10 minutes. Add the half-and-half, cheese and flour, mixing well. Let simmer until thickened and cheese is melted and creamy.

We like it served over broccoli or a baked potato.

SHRIMP COUBION

SERVES 5 TO 7

With this recipe it's best to use fresh Gulf shrimp. We catch our own shrimp so they are always fresh straight out of the Gulf of Mexico. When you buy shrimp, they should not be orange or pink but rather a light brown or cloudy clear color. I also prefer to use a small to medium shrimp with this recipe. If all I have are large shrimp, I dice them into smaller pieces.

1 1/2 tablespoons vegetable oil

1 large onion, diced

1 large bell pepper, diced

1 teaspoon minced garlic

1 (10-ounce) can Mild Rotel Diced Tomatoes and Green Chilies

2 (10-ounce) cans cream

of mushroom soup

3 cups water

1/2 teaspoon salt

2 tablespoons Gatorqueen's Bayou Seasoning

2 pounds small or medium shrimp, peeled

4 cups cooked rice

In a large pot on medium heat, add the vegetable oil, onions, bell peppers, minced garlic, and Rotel, and stir often until onions and bell peppers are soft, wilted, and slightly brown. Once that is done add the soup, water, salt, and Bayou seasoning, and continue cooking on medium heat for about 30 minutes, stirring occasionally. Once your gravy begins to thicken, add your shrimp and let it cook for 10 more minutes.

Serve coubion over rice with small sweet peas, and baked bread rolls on the side.

CRAWFISH AU GRATIN

SERVES 6 TO 8

2 pounds Louisiana crawfish tails

1 stick butter

1 large onion, finely diced

1 large bell pepper, finely diced

1 teaspoon minced garlic

1 rib celery, finely diced

$1/2$ teaspoon parsley flakes

$1/4$ teaspoon salt

$1/2$ teaspoon black pepper

$1/4$ teaspoon cayenne pepper

$1/4$ teaspoon Gatorqueen's Bayou Seasoning

2 cups water

4 cups half-and-half

1 pound Velveeta cheese, cut into small cubes

2 tablespoons flour

Rinse your crawfish and set aside.

In a medium pot, melt the butter and add the onions, peppers, garlic, celery, and parsley. Sauté this for 10 to 12 minutes on low heat, until mixture is wilted. Add the crawfish, stir well, then add salt, pepper, cayenne, Bayou seasoning, and water. Let this cook for 15 minutes, until water is absorbed. Then add the half-and-half, cheese, and flour, stirring constantly to incorporate cheese and flour. Let this simmer for 10 minutes, or until cheese has melted. Best served over baked or fried fish.

SEAFOOD GUMBO

SERVES 8 TO 10

In Louisiana, gumbo is always on our minds. Especially when the first cold front comes in, it's gumbo weather.

1 cup flour

1 cup oil

1 large onion, diced

1 large bell pepper, diced

2 tablespoons minced garlic

4 quarts water

1 teaspoon parsley flakes

1 bay leaf

1/4 cup gumbo filé

1 (10-ounce) can Mild Rotel Diced

Tomatoes and Green Chilies

1 teaspoon salt

1/4 teaspoon black pepper

1 tablespoon Gatorqueen's Bayou Seasoning

1 pound medium Gulf shrimp

1 pound crawfish tails

1 pound dark claw crabmeat

3 green onions, sliced thin

6 cups cooked rice

In a large pot, start making your roux by mixing together the flour and oil. Cook over medium heat, stirring constantly until browned. Remove from heat and set aside to cool for about 10 minutes. Place the pot back on medium heat and add the onions, peppers, and garlic to the roux, cooking and stirring until vegetables are wilted. Add the water, stirring constantly over medium heat to break up the roux. Then add parsley, bay leaf, filé, Rotel, salt, pepper, and Bayou seasoning. Let this cook for 1 hour.

Add your seafood and green onions. Cook for 20 minutes. Season to taste.

Best served over a small amount of rice with a lot of gravy, and potato salad on the side.

CRAWFISH SALAD

SERVES 6 TO 8

We've heard these called, crawdads, mud bugs, crawdaddies, and other names. But in Louisiana we call them crawfish. No matter what anyone calls them, they are good. Get into your kitchen and make it your own. I use a food processor to mince the vegetables.

3 cups water

2 pounds crawfish tails

8 large boiled eggs

$1/2$ cup minced onions

$1/2$ cup minced bell pepper

$1/4$ cup minced garlic

$1/4$ cup minced green onions

1 teaspoon parsley flakes

1 tablespoon Gatorqueen's Bayou Seasoning

$1/2$ teaspoon salt

$1/2$ teaspoon celery salt

1 teaspoon prepared mustard

$2 1/2$ cups mayonnaise

In a medium-sized pot, boil your crawfish in 3 cups water for 10 minutes, then strain.

Peel the boiled eggs and place them to the side with your crawfish. Mince your crawfish finely in a food processor or blender, and place in a large bowl. Do the same with the eggs. Mince the onions, peppers, garlic, green onions, and parsley flakes with all the spices, then add to your bowl. Add the mayonnaise and mix well.

Can be eaten on a sandwich or with crackers.

CRAB SALAD

SERVES 16 TO 20

A food processor and microwave make quick work of this recipe preparation.

4 pounds white crabmeat

2 tablespoons vegetable oil

1 (8-ounce) package cream cheese

6 large boiled eggs

$1/4$ cup minced onion

$1/4$ cup minced bell pepper

$1/4$ cup minced garlic

$1/4$ cup minced green onions

1 teaspoon parsley flakes

1 tablespoon Gatorqueen's Bayou Seasoning

$1/2$ teaspoon salt

$1/2$ teaspoon prepared mustard

1 cup mayonnaise

Pick through the crabmeat with your fingers to make sure there are no peelings or shells.

Heat the oil in a skillet and sauté the crabmeat for 2–3 minutes, then set aside in a bowl.

Melt the cream cheese in the microwave and add to your crab. Mince boiled eggs well in your food processor, and stir into the crab. In a food processor, mince onions, peppers, garlic, and green onions together, then add the mixture to the crab. Add all the seasonings, mustard, and mayonnaise. Mix together well, and your crab salad is done.

Good served with crackers, or great to top a green salad!

CHICKEN

BAKED CHICKEN

SERVES 4

1 whole chicken, cut into quarters

1 tablespoon Worcestershire sauce

1 teaspoon prepared mustard

2 tablespoons Gatorqueen's Bayou Seasoning

2 tablespoons parsley flakes

1 teaspoon salt

$1/2$ teaspoon black pepper

1 stick butter

Preheat oven to 350 degrees.

Place the chicken, Worcestershire sauce, mustard, Bayou seasoning, parsley, salt, and pepper into a large bowl and toss to coat the chicken well. Place chicken into a 9 x 13-inch pan Cut the butter into thin strips and spread over your chicken. Bake uncovered for 1 hour and 40 minutes, or until chicken is tender and golden on top.

Best served with creamed potatoes and small sweet peas.

SMOTHERED CHICKEN

SERVES 5 TO 7

1 whole chicken, cut up

1 tablespoon parsley flakes

1$^1/_2$ tablespoons Gatorqueen's Bayou Seasoning

1 tablespoon prepared mustard

1 tablespoon Worcestershire sauce

1 stick butter

1 large onion, diced

1 medium bell pepper, diced

2 tablespoons minced garlic

4 cups water

4 cups cooked rice

Place chicken pieces in a medium bowl, and add the parsley, Bayou seasoning, mustard, and Worcestershire sauce; mix well, and place aside.

In a large pot over medium heat, add the butter, onions, bell peppers, and garlic and cook, stirring often until onions, and peppers are wilted and golden brown. Add the contents of your bowl with the chicken to the pot and continue cooking over medium heat until chicken is browned, stirring occasionally for about 15 minutes. Add water and continue cooking over medium heat stirring occasionally until water is mostly boiled out, and a semi-thick darker gravy remains. Serve over rice with small sweet peas, bread rolls, and a green salad on the side.

FRIED CHICKEN

SERVES 4 TO 6

2 large eggs, beaten

1 (12-ounce) can evaporated milk

2 tablespoons prepared mustard

1 tablespoon Worcestershire sauce

2 tablespoons Gatorqueen's Bayou Seasoning

1 teaspoon salt

1 teaspoon black pepper

2 tablespoons parsley flakes

1 whole fryer chicken cut into quarters or several pieces

6 cups vegetable oil

6 cups all-purpose flour

In a large bowl, beat together the eggs, milk, mustard, Worcestershire sauce, Bayou seasoning, salt, pepper, and parsley. Add your chicken, coat well, and refrigerate for at least 30 minutes.

Place the vegetable oil in a large skillet and heat to 375 degrees. In a large bowl, add the flour and begin adding the chicken one piece at a time, covering chicken pieces entirely with flour. Batter as many pieces as your skillet can hold with pieces barely touching or not touching at all. Add chicken to the hot oil and let cook on each side for 10–15 minutes (make sure the chicken is golden brown on each side). Place fried chicken onto paper towels to drain. Chicken should be juicy on the inside and crunchy on the outside.

Great served with creamed potatoes, coleslaw, and your choice of beans.

CHICKEN FRICASSEE

SERVES 4 TO 5

A lot of Cajun meals in south Louisiana are made with a roux, which is 1 cup all-purpose flour, and 1 cup vegetable oil. This is cooked on low heat by stirring constantly with a spatula until your roux gets dark brown for stews, gumbos, etc. Using a spatula makes it easy to move the roux around in your pot so it doesn't burn.

1 whole chicken, cut up

1 cup oil, divided

1 cup all-purpose flour

8 cups water

1 large onion, diced

1 large bell pepper, diced

2 tablespoons minced garlic

3 green onions, diced

1 teaspoon Louisiana Hot Sauce

3 tablespoons Gatorqueen's Bayou Seasoning

1 teaspoon salt

3 tablespoons ketchup

1 pinch black pepper

Place chicken pieces into a bowl, and set aside. Heat $1/2$ cup oil in a large skillet and brown the chicken on all sides, then remove from oil and set aside.

In the same skillet, add remaining $1/2$ cup oil and the flour. Cook and stir over medium heat until you have brown roux. Add the water, stirring as you pour. Add the onions, peppers, garlic, green onions, and seasonings, stirring constantly to break up the roux. Cook over medium heat for $1 1/2$ hours. Then add the chicken, and cook for 1 hour, stirring occasionally, until the liquid cooks out and the stew thickens.

Serve over hot rice with potato salad on the side.

CHICKEN AND SAUSAGE GUMBO

SERVES 8 TO 10

Any gumbo tastes better when you prepare your own roux. The process is simple.

$1/2$ stick butter

2 pounds fresh or smoked pork sausage

2 whole chickens, cut up

1 cup vegetable oil

1 cup all-purpose flour

1 large onion, diced

1 large bell pepper, diced

$1/2$ cup diced green onions

$1/2$ teaspoon parsley flakes

2 tablespoons minced garlic

4 quarts water

1 bay leaf

$1/4$ teaspoon gumbo filé

1 teaspoon salt

$1/4$ teaspoon black pepper

1 tablespoon Gatorqueen's Bayou Seasoning

5 cups cooked rice

In a large skillet over medium heat, add the butter and sausage. Brown the sausage until cooked through, then remove from skillet and cut it into 1-inch slices. Set aside.

In the same skillet begin browning your chicken for about 10 minutes and then set aside with the sausage.

In a large pot add the oil and flour, stirring continuously on a low heat, preferably with a flat spatula, until the flour has turned a dark brown color. This is your roux. In the same pot, add the onions, peppers, green onions, parsley, and garlic to the roux and continue to stir constantly for about 5 more minutes. Add the 4 quarts of water, stirring until roux is mixed well with the other ingredients. Cook over medium heat, bringing to a slow boil. Add the bay leaf, filé, salt, pepper, and Bayou seasoning. Cook this on a low-to-medium heat for another 30 minutes.

Add your chicken to the pot and continue cooking for about 40 more minutes. Finally add your sausage and continue cooking for another 15 minutes. Add more seasoning to your taste if needed.

Serve over rice with a lot of gravy and potato salad on the side.

OVEN-STYLE BARBEQUE CHICKEN

SERVES 4 TO 6

$1/2$ stick butter

1 (12-ounce) bottle Jack Miller's Bar-B-Que Sauce

1 whole chicken, quartered

2 tablespoons parsley flakes

1 teaspoon salt

1 tablespoon prepared mustard

1 tablespoon Worcestershire sauce

Preheat oven to 375 degrees.

Place the butter in a microwave-safe bowl and heat until melted. Add the barbeque sauce and stir together.

Place the chicken in a bowl and add the parsley, salt, mustard and Worcestershire sauce; mix well to coat the chicken.

Place your chicken in a large ungreased baking pan and cover with the barbeque sauce mixture. Bake uncovered for 1 hour and 30 minutes. Serve with potato salad and baked beans

CHICKEN FETTUCCINE

SERVES 8

In our house chicken is the only meat we buy from the grocery store. It's quick, easy and good. Got to have my chicken.

1 stick butter

1 large onion, diced

1 large bell pepper, diced

1 tablespoon minced garlic

$1/4$ cup dried jalapeño peppers (seeds removed)

$1/2$ rib celery, finely diced

2 tablespoons parsley flakes

4 large boneless, skinless chicken breasts, diced

2 cups water

1 (10-ounce) can cream of mushroom soup

2 cups half-and-half

2 pounds Velveeta block cheese, diced

1 tablespoon Gatorqueen's Bayou Seasoning

2 (16-ounce) packages fettuccine noodles

Melt the butter in a large pot over medium heat. Add the onions, pepper, garlic, jalapeños, celery, and parsley flakes. Wilt down the vegetables until browned, then add the chicken. Cook and stir mixture for 10 minutes, or until chicken is browned. Add water and continue cooking for 25 minutes.

Turn heat to low, add soup, half-and-half, Velveeta and Bayou seasoning. Stir mixture together well and let it cook down slowly, stirring occasionally so cheese doesn't stick.

Meanwhile, cook noodles according to package directions; drain well and add fold into the cheese mixture. Cook for 10 minutes, until thick and creamy.

CHICKEN SPAGHETTI

SERVES 7 TO 10

$^1/_2$ cup all-purpose flour

$^1/_2$ cup vegetable oil

2 quarts water

1 large onion, diced

1 large bell pepper, diced

1 tablespoon minced garlic

1 tablespoon parsley flakes

2 tablespoons Gatorqueen's Bayou Seasoning

2 (15-ounce) cans tomato sauce

1 (10-ounce) can Mild Rotel Diced
Tomatoes and Green Chilies

2 whole chickens, deboned and cut into pieces

1 pound thin spaghetti noodles, cooked and drained

In a large pot, add the flour and oil and cook over low heat, stirring constantly until flour is dark brown to make a small roux. Add the water to your roux, along with the onions, peppers, garlic, parsley, Bayou seasoning, tomato sauce, and Rotel, stirring well. Cook over low heat for 1 hour. Then add your chicken, and cook over medium heat for 1 hour. You may have to add a little more water if the sauce thickens too much. Add the noodles to the pot and let cook, stirring occasionally, for another 15 minutes, or until your sauce is semi-thick

Serve with baked garlic bread.

CHICKEN ENCHILADAS

SERVES 6 TO 8

3 pounds boneless, skinless chicken breast

4 small cubes chicken bouillon

1 stick butter

1 large red bell pepper, diced

1 large onion, diced

2 tablespoons minced garlic

1 tablespoon dried cilantro

1 tablespoon cumin

1 tablespoon Gatorqueen's Bayou Seasoning

2 (8-ounce) packages cream cheese

2 cups cooked rice

1 (10-ounce) jar green salsa verde

1 (8-count) package flour tortillas

1 (10-ounce) can green chile enchilada sauce

1 (16-oounce) bag shredded American cheese

Place chicken and bouillon cubes in a medium pot and cover with water to by $1/2$ inch. Place a lid one the pot and bring to a boil; let cook for 25 minutes. Strain your chicken and reserve the stock for later use. Cut the chicken into small $1/2$-inch cubes and place to the side.

In a large pot over medium heat, add the butter, red peppers, onions, garlic, and cilantro, and cook this down for 20 minutes, stirring frequently. Add the cubed chicken, cumin, Bayou seasoning, and 1 cup of the reserved chicken stock, and continue cooking over a low heat for another 5 minutes. Add the cream cheese, stirring and mixing slowly until semi-thick. Next, add the cooked rice, mixing in well; remove from heat and set aside.

Preheat oven to 350 degrees.

Lightly coat the bottom of a 9 x 13-inch pan with the salsa verde. To assemble the enchiladas, take each tortilla and fill the center with the chicken and rice mixture. Roll it closed and place it in the pan. Repeat with the other tortillas and lay them side by side in the pan. Pour the remaining enchilada sauce over the top of your filled tortillas, then sprinkle the cheese evenly over the top. Bake in the oven until the sauce is bubbly and the cheese has completely melted.

CHICKEN TORTILLA WRAPS

SERVES 8

This is a three-skillet meal preparation. Otherwise, you will need to clean a hot skillet before proceeding.

1/2 cup oil, divided

16 chicken breast tenders

2 tablespoons Gatorqueen's Bayou Seasoning

1 teaspoon prepared mustard

1 tablespoon Worcestershire sauce

1 large onion, diced

1 large bell pepper, diced

2 tablespoons minced garlic

2 tablespoons parsley flakes

1 cup water

1 (8-count) package flour tortillas

2 cups shredded lettuce

1 large tomato, diced

1 (8-ounce) package mild shredded cheese

1 package Marketside Chunky Avocado

Preheat 1/4 cup oil in a large skillet.

Place chicken tenders into a large bowl and add the Bayou seasoning, mustard, and Worcestershire sauce; mix well. Place seasoned tenders in hot oil and brown on each side until cooked through. Remove and let drain on a paper towel.

In a separate skillet, heat remaining 1/4 cup of oil and add the onions, peppers, garlic, and parsley flakes. Wilt this down for 15 minutes and then add your chicken and water; cook this down until water has cooked out and you have a thick gravy.

Prepare another skillet with cooking spray and heat the tortillas on each side. Add 2 chicken tenders to each tortilla along with cooked onions, peppers, and gravy. Top with lettuce, tomato, cheese, and avocado. Wrap these up tightly and serve.

CHICKEN SOUP

SERVES 8 TO 10

On cold days in south Louisiana I like to make chicken soup. Any leftovers we have go into the freezer for the next cold day.

$1/4$ cup oil

2 whole chickens, cut up

$1/2$ stick butter

1 large onion, diced

1 large bell pepper, diced

2 tablespoons minced garlic

8 cups water

2 tablespoons Gatorqueen's Bayou Seasoning

2 cups cut and diced cabbage

1 (14-ounce) can green beans

1 (15-ounce) can whole kernel corn

1 (14-ounce) can sliced carrots

2 (15-ounce) cans tomato sauce

1 cup uncooked rice

2 large white potatoes, diced

1 (16-ounce) package thin spaghetti
noodles, broken in half

Heat the oil in a large skillet, then add the chicken pieces and brown on each side. Remove from oil and set aside.

In a large pot, melt the butter and brown the onions, peppers, and garlic until caramelized. Add the chicken and water. Add Bayou seasoning, cabbage, green beans, corn, carrots, and tomato sauce. Let this cook for 25 minutes, then add the rice, potatoes, and noodles. Let this all cook down for 30 minutes on low heat. Serve with crackers.

CHICKEN SALAD

SERVES 8 TO 10

12 large boiled eggs

10 chicken leg quarters

8 cups water

$^1/_2$ cup diced onion

$^1/_2$ cup diced bell pepper

$^1/_4$ cup minced garlic

$^1/_4$ cup diced green onions

1 teaspoon parsley flakes

1 tablespoon Gatorqueen's Bayou Seasoning

$^1/_2$ teaspoon salt

$^1/_2$ teaspoon celery salt

1 tablespoon prepared mustard

$2^1/_2$ cups mayonnaise

Peel the boiled eggs, chop them in a food processor, and place them into a large bowl; set aside.

In a large pot, boil your chicken in the 8 cups of water for 25–30 minutes. Once the chicken is cooked, remove from pot and place into a separate dish to cool. When cool enough to handle, debone your chicken and add it to the food processor; chop it well, and then add it to the bowl with the eggs.

Add the onions, bell peppers, garlic, and green onions to the bowl of the food processor, blend well, and add to the chicken and eggs. Finally, add the parsley flakes, Bayou seasoning, salt, celery salt, mustard, and mayonnaise and mix everything together very well.

Serve as a sandwich with bread or as a dip with crackers.

CHICKEN JAMBALAYA

SERVES 6 TO 8

2 pounds boneless, skinless chicken

1 1/2 sticks butter

2 medium onions, diced

1 large bell pepper, diced

1 rib celery, diced fine

1 tablespoon minced garlic

1/2 cup green onions, diced fine

2 tablespoons Gatorqueen's Bayou Seasoning

1 tablespoon Worcestershire sauce

1 teaspoon Savoie's Dark Roux

1 teaspoon ketchup

6 cups water

3 cups cooked rice

Cut the chicken into 1-inch pieces and set aside.

In a large pot over medium heat, add the butter, onions, bell peppers, celery, garlic, and green onions and cook down, stirring often for about 25 minutes, or until vegetables are wilted and golden brown. Add your chicken to the pot and continue to stir often while chicken browns down with the rest of the ingredients. If the ingredients begin to stick before the chicken is browned, you can add about 1/4 cup of water and mix well.

Now add Bayou seasoning, Worcestershire sauce, roux, ketchup and water and mix well. Let this cook for about 40 minutes over medium-to-medium-high heat until the liquids have cooked down to about 1 inch of gravy. At this point add the cooked rice and cook on a low-to-medium heat, stirring frequently, so the rice can absorb the gravy. Turn the heat off and let simmer for about 10 minutes. Your jambalaya should be moist, but not runny.

Delicious served with black-eyed peas, and coleslaw.

ALLIGATOR

FRIED ALLIGATOR NUGGETS

SERVES 5 TO 7

When cooking alligator, the most important thing to remember is to remove all of the fat from the meat before you cook it. The fat leaves a bad flavor much like fish oil (or blood in fish filets). Also, just like any other wild game, it is usually better to marinate your meat before preparing your recipe.

2 pounds gator meat

3 large eggs, beaten

1 cup half-n-half

2 tablespoons prepared mustard

2 tablespoons Worcestershire sauce

2 tablespoons Gatorqueen's Bayou Seasoning

2 cups vegetable oil

2 cups all-purpose flour

Cut your meat into small cube-sized nuggets about 1 x $^1/_2$ inch thick.

Next, mix the eggs, half-n-half, mustard, Worcestershire sauce, and seasoning in a large bowl, stirring well. Add your meat to the mix and let marinate for about 1$^1/_2$ hours.

When you are ready to fry the nuggets, pour the vegetable oil into a large skillet or frying pan and heat to 375 degrees.

Add the flour into a large bowl. Take each piece of meat and roll in the flour, covering completely. Add the floured meat to the hot oil in batches. Be sure not to cook too many pieces at once; leave enough room so the meat pieces are slightly separated. Cook until golden brown all the way around each piece. Remove fried alligator nuggets from the oil and let drain on paper towels in a separate pan or dish; continue the process until all of your meat is cooked.

Best served with fried potatoes.

ALLIGATOR FRICASSEE

SERVES 8 TO 10

Always remember when you are cooking alligator to remove all the fat, because this will make your food taste bad. Just know when you get your alligator meat, check it carefully, then you are good to cook away.

1 cup vegetable oil

1 cup all-purpose flour

4–6 cups water, divided

2 cups finely diced celery

1 large onion, diced

1 large bell pepper, diced

1 teaspoon minced garlic

1/4 cup ketchup

1 teaspoon hot sauce

1 tablespoon Gatorqueen's Bayou Seasoning

1/2 teaspoon pepper

1/2 teaspoon salt

3 pounds alligator meat, cut into 1-inch cubes

2 cups cooked rice

In a large pot heat the oil on low heat, adding the flour to make roux. Cook and stir until browned. Then add 4 cups water, stirring until roux breaks up. Add the celery, onion, peppers, garlic, ketchup, hot sauce, and seasonings. Cook this down for 1 hour on low heat, then add remaining 2 cups of water and your meat. Cook this for 40 minutes, until thick and the alligator meat is tender.

Serve over cooked rice or with a side of stuffed potato.

ALLIGATOR ÉTOUFFÉE

SERVES 5 TO 7

2 pounds gator meat

3 tablespoons Gatorqueen's Bayou Seasoning

1 stick butter

2 medium onions, diced

1 large bell pepper, diced

1 rib celery, diced fine

3 tablespoons minced garlic

2 tablespoons parsley flakes

1 (10-ounce) can Mild Rotel Diced
Tomatoes and Green Chilies

2 cups water

2 (10-) cans cream of mushroom soup

4 cups cooked rice

Cut your meat into small cube-like pieces, about 1 x $^1/_2$ inch thick. Place the meat into a bowl and add the Bayou seasoning; mix well.

In a large pot over medium heat, add butter and let it melt down. Now add the onions, peppers, celery, garlic, parsley, and Rotel and continue cooking over low-to-medium heat for about 30 minutes, stirring often. You may have to occasionally add a little water to keep ingredients from sticking to the pot. Add your gator meat and stir while meat browns down with the rest of the ingredients. Once meat is browned and vegetables are wilted and golden brown, add the water and soup. Cook over medium heat for another 25–30 minutes, stirring occasionally, or until your gravy is semi-thick.

Serve over rice with your choice of beans and baked bread rolls.

SMOTHERED ALLIGATOR

SERVES 5 TO 7

In south Louisiana, September is alligator season. Harvesting gators is a wetlands conservation measure, helping to prevent overpopulation. Nothing goes to waste, especially the meat. It is a delicacy all over the country.

2 pounds alligator meat (dark or white), cut into 1-inch cubes

1/2 cup evaporated milk

1 teaspoon D.a.T. Sauce (all natural hot sauce)

2 tablespoons Gatorqueen's Bayou Seasoning

1/2 teaspoon salt

1/4 teaspoon black pepper

1/3 cup oil

2 medium onions, diced

1 large bell pepper, diced

1 tablespoon minced garlic

1 tablespoon parsley flakes

1 (10-ounce) can Mild Rotel Diced Tomatoes and Green Chilies

1 (10-ounce) can cream of mushroom soup

4 cups water

2 cups cooked rice

Place your gator meat in a bowl and add milk, D.a.T. sauce, Bayou seasoning, salt, and pepper; mix well and place to side for 30 minutes.

In a large deep skillet, add the oil, onions, peppers, garlic, parsley, and Rotel. Cook until vegetables are wilted. Add your alligator meat and brown along with the onions. Add soup and water. Cook over medium heat for 1 1/2 hours, until water is absorbed and you are left with a thick gravy.

Serve over rice with sweet peas on the side.

ALLIGATOR SAUCE PIQUANT

SERVES 8 TO 10

4 pounds alligator meat

1 cup vegetable oil

1 cup all-purpose flour

2 large onions, diced

1 large bell pepper, diced

2 tablespoons minced garlic

1/2 cup sliced green onions

1 (10-ounce) can Mild Rotel Diced
Tomatoes and Green Chilies

1 (4-ounce) can mushroom pieces and stems

8 cups water

1 (15-ounce) can tomato sauce

1/2 cup ketchup

1 tablespoon hot sauce

3 tablespoons Gatorqueen's Bayou Seasoning

1 teaspoon salt

1/2 teaspoon black pepper

2 cups cooked rice

Cut your alligator into 1-inch cubes and place to the aside. In a large Magnalite or another large oval pot over low heat, add the vegetable oil and flour. Stir together to make a roux and cook until flour is a peanut butter color. Stir in the onions, peppers, garlic, green onions, Rotel and mushrooms. Cook until the vegetables are wilted, then add the water, stirring to break up the roux. Cook over medium heat until this starts to boil. Add tomato sauce, ketchup, hot sauce, Bayou seasoning, salt, and pepper. Stir well, then add your gator meat. Cook your Sauce Piquant for 1 hour and 30 minutes, checking to make sure the meat is tender. Your gravy should be thick and flavorful.

Serve over hot rice with white beans and potato salad on the side.

ALLIGATOR COUBION

SERVES 5 TO 7

Whenever preparing alligator meat, always be sure to remove all fat from the meat. The fat will give the meat an undesirable flavor. Without the fat the alligator meat is quite tasty.

2 pounds gator meat

$1/3$ cup whole milk

$1/4$ cup Worcestershire sauce

1 cup Italian dressing

2 tablespoons Gatorqueen's Bayou Seasoning

2 tablespoons olive oil

$1^1/2$ large onions, diced

1 large bell pepper, diced

1 tablespoon minced garlic

$1/2$ teaspoon celery salt

1 (10-ounce) can Mild Rotel Diced Tomatoes and Green Chilies

2 (10-ounce) cans of cream of mushroom soup

3 cups water

4 cups cooked rice

Cut your meat into small pieces about 1 inch long and $1/2$-inch thick. Place meat into a large bowl along with the milk, Worcestershire sauce, Italian dressing, and Bayou seasoning; mix well. Set aside and let marinate for 1 hour.

In a large pot over medium-to-high heat, add the olive oil, onions, bell peppers, garlic, celery salt, and Rotel; cook down, stirring often, until vegetables are soft, wilted and golden brown.

Strain the alligator meat and add to the pot. Brown the meat, stirring often over medium heat for about 15 minutes. Stir in the soup and water and continue to cook over medium heat for another hour, stirring occasionally, until your gravy is thick; do not cover with a lid.

Serve over rice with your choice of beans and baked bread rolls.

ALLIGATOR PATTIES

SERVES 6 TO 7

These can be eaten on a sandwich with mayo, lettuce, tomato, mustard, and Cajun dip. Or just eat them like they are. Yummy! A food processor will help the preparation go faster.

2 pounds alligator jowl meat (cheeks)

2 medium onions, cut into chunks

1 large red bell pepper, seeded and cut into chunks

1 teaspoon minced garlic

2 medium red potatoes, quartered

1–2-inch piece of carrot

4–5 green onions

2 large eggs

1 tablespoon parsley flakes

2 tablespoons Gatorqueen's Bayou Seasoning

$1/2$ teaspoon celery salt

1 tablespoon Worcestershire sauce

1 teaspoon prepared mustard

1 cup Italian-style breadcrumbs

1 teaspoon D.a.T. sauce

3 cups vegetable oil

Mince gator meat very well in a food processor, then place into a large bowl. Put to the side.

To the bowl of your food process, add onions, peppers, garlic, potatoes, carrot, green onions, and eggs and process to mince vegetables well. Add this to your meat. Add parsley flakes, Bayou Seasoning, celery salt, Worcestershire, mustard, breadcrumbs and D.a.T. sauce. Incorporate this mixture using both hands; get in there and mix and fold.

Heat oil to 350–375 degrees in a deep skillet over medium heat. Shape your patties and fry a few at a time until golden brown on once side, then flip and fry other side. Repeat until all the patties are done. Drain on paper towels.

DUCK

STUFFED DUCK WRAPS

SERVES 10

On Pecan Island during the yearly duck hunting season, it seems like the island sinks a few inches, with all the hunters coming down to enjoy the privilege of shooting ducks. The stuffed duck breasts wrapped in bacon are south Louisiana comfort food; just pass the tray around and grab wraps!

20 teal breasts, skinless

1 (12-ounce) bottle Italian salad dressing

3 tablespoons Worcestershire sauce

2 tablespoons Gator Queen's Bayou Seasoning

1 teaspoon hot sauce

2 (8-ounce) packages cream cheese

2 pounds thick-sliced bacon

1 (8-ounce) jar sliced jalapeños

Prepare the grill or fire pit with charcoal, but wait to light; you have to marinate the duck first.

Cut duck breasts in half, then cut a pocket down the middle for the cream cheese and jalapeños. Place the cut breasts in a large bowl and pour in the Italian dressing. Add Worcestershire, Bayou seasoning, and hot sauce and marinate for 2 hours. Soak 30 toothpicks in water for 10 minutes.

Cut the cream cheese into cubes. Lay strips of bacon on a cutting board, place 1 duck breast down on each strip at least 1 inch from one end of bacon, and then stuff with cream cheese and at least 2–3 jalapeño slices. Then wrap the stuffed breast tightly with the bacon strip and stick a toothpick through to hold it together. Repeat until all the breasts have been stuffed and wrapped.

While you are making the wraps, light your charcoal. Once your wraps are ready and charcoal is white, put wraps on your grate or grill, letting one side get good and crispy and then flipping to the other side. These wraps are so good you can just pop them in your mouth.

Serve as a comfort food, just pass the tray around and grab wraps!

DUCK FRICASSEE

SERVES 8 TO 10

1 cup flour
1 1/3 cups oil, divided
15 duck breasts (no skin)
1 large onion, diced
1 large bell pepper, diced
2 tablespoons minced garlic
2 green onions, sliced
6–8 cups water, divided

1 (10-ounce) can Mild Rotel Diced Tomatoes and Green Chilies
2 tablespoons ketchup
1 teaspoon mustard
2 tablespoons Worcestershire sauce
2 tablespoons Gatorqueen's Bayou Seasoning
1/4 teaspoon salt
2 cups cooked rice

In a large pot, use flour and 1 cup oil to make peanut butter–colored roux; set it aside to cool.

Cut your duck breasts into 1-inch cubes and place into a bowl. Heat 1/3 cup oil in a skillet, and add onions, peppers, garlic, and green onions. When the mixture is wilted, transfer vegetables into the roux, keeping the oil in the skillet. Mix vegetables into the roux. Add 2 cups of water, and cook on low heat.

In your skillet, brown the duck meat and then add to the roux. Add the Rotel, ketchup, mustard, Worcestershire sauce, Bayou seasoning, salt, and the 4–6 cups water, to cover. Cook this down on low heat for 1 hour and 30 minutes, checking to see if the duck is tender. You may need to add more seasoning to taste. If your fricassee gets too thick before your duck is tender, just add 1/2 cup water. It should then be the perfect consistency and the duck should be very tender.

Served over hot cooked rice and potato salad, with white beans on the side.

SMOTHERED DUCK

SERVES 4 TO 6

$^1/_3$ cup vegetable oil

1 large onion, diced

1 large bell pepper, diced

1 tablespoon minced garlic

10 duck breasts (no skin), diced

2 tablespoons parsley flakes

1 tablespoon prepared mustard

1 tablespoon Worcestershire sauce

2 tablespoons Gator Queen's Bayou Seasoning

1 teaspoon hot sauce

4 cups water

1 (10-ounce) can cream of mushroom soup

In a medium pot, heat the oil and add the onions, peppers, and garlic. Wilt this down and let it caramelize to a brown color.

In a large bowl, mix duck meat, parsley, mustard, Worcestershire sauce, Bayou seasoning, and hot sauce, then pour this on top of the onions. Cook until the meat is well browned. Then add water and soup. Cook this down for 1 hour and 40 minutes, depending on how fast the duck breast gets tender.

Serve over rice with a green bean casserole on the side.

FRIED DUCK

SERVES 4 TO 6

5 large duck breasts, skin on

2 cups half-n-half

2 teaspoons Gatorqueen's Bayou Seasoning

$^1/_2$ teaspoon salt

1 tablespoon prepared mustard

1 tablespoon Worcestershire sauce

1 teaspoon hot sauce

1 tablespoon parsley flakes

3 cups oil

4 cups all-purpose flour

To slice duck breasts in half, carefully lay the breast flat, and slide your knife through the breast parallel to the cutting surface to make 2 duck filets. Afterwards, the breast should have skin on one side and no skin on the other. Place the fillets into a bowl, and add half-n-half, Bayou seasoning, salt, mustard, Worcestershire sauce, hot sauce, and parsley. Marinate for 3 hours.

Heat oil in a large skillet. Press breast fillets into the flour to coat, shake off any excess flour, and then fry to a golden brown on both sides. Repeat until all duck breasts are deep-fried. Place to drain on paper towels.

Serve with stuffed potatoes.

DUCK SAUCE PIQUANT

SERVES 8 TO 10

4 tablespoons vegetable oil

4 tablespoons flour

2 medium onions, chopped

1 large bell pepper, chopped

1 tablespoon minced garlic

2 ribs celery, finely chopped

2 (6-ounce) cans tomato paste

1 teaspoon sugar

1 (8-ounce) can Mild Rotel Diced Tomatoes and Green Chilies

10 large duck breasts (skin off), diced

2 cups chicken stock

2 cups water

1/2 cup green onions, chopped

1 tablespoon parsley flakes

1 teaspoon hot sauce

Salt and pepper to taste

Red pepper to taste

2 cups cooked rice

In a large saucepan, heat oil and flour, stirring constantly to make a roux. Add the onions, peppers, garlic, and celery, letting this simmer for 5 minutes. Add tomato paste, sugar, and Rotel; simmer on low heat for 10 minutes. Add the breast meat, chicken stock, and water, stirring well.

Add the green onions, parsley, and hot sauce. Season your gravy to your taste using salt, pepper, and red pepper. Cook for 1 1/2 hours.

Serve over rice with potato salad on the side.

DUCK COUBION

SERVES 6 TO 8

$^1/_2$ stick butter

1 large onion, diced

1 large bell pepper, diced

1 teaspoon garlic, minced

1 (10-ounce) can Mild Rotel Diced
Tomatoes and Green Chilies

2 pounds skinless duck breast, diced

2 (10-ounce) cans of cream of celery soup

2 tablespoons Gatorqueen's Bayou Seasoning

$^1/_2$ teaspoon salt

3 cups water

In a large pot on medium heat, mix butter, onion, peppers, garlic, and Rotel. Stir often until vegetables are wilted and brown. Add the duck breast meat and brown. Once browned, add the soup, Bayou seasoning, salt, and water. Cook this down on medium heat for 1 hour and 15 minutes, until it is thickened and the duck is tender.

Serve over rice and stuffed potatoes.

NUTRIA, RABBIT, SQUIRREL, AND TURTLE

SMOTHERED NUTRIA

SERVES 6

Remember, the nutria is a vegetarian, so this meat is lean and healthy.

8 nutria legs, deboned and diced

1 stick of butter

2 medium onions, diced

1 large bell pepper, diced

1 tablespoon minced garlic

1 tablespoon parsley flakes

1 teaspoon hot sauce

2 tablespoons Gatorqueen's Bayou Seasoning

1 teaspoon prepared mustard

2 tablespoons Worcestershire sauce

Salt and pepper to taste

4 cups water

2 cups cooked rice

Place the deboned meat into a bowl.

Melt butter in a large pot and add onions, peppers and garlic. Wilt this down and caramelize until golden brown. Add parsley flakes, hot sauce, Bayou Seasoning, mustard, Worcestershire sauce, and salt and pepper and stir well.

Add meat to the onions. Smother this down with onions and cook meat until brown, then add water. Cook this for 1 hour and 30 minutes, until all water is absorbed and meat is tender.

Serve this meal over hot cooked rice with some red beans on the side.

FRIED NUTRIA

SERVES 6

Every year there is a bounty placed on nutria from November until March. These animals were once sold for pelts and meat. Now the bounty is a placed as a conservation effort to save the wetlands. The nutria is known to be vegetarian and has a nasty reputation for eating everything in sight that is green. My family traps nutria and sells the tails for conservation counting, but we keep the meat for cooking purposes. My brothers, sister and I all grew up eating nutria. My mom and dad have been trapping these animals since the 1970s.

If available, the best part of nutria for frying is the back legs.

2 large eggs

2 cups evaporated milk

1 tablespoon Gatorqueen's Bayou Seasoning

$1/2$ teaspoon salt

1 pinch black pepper

1 tablespoon mustard

1 tablespoon Worcestershire sauce

1 teaspoon hot sauce

6 legs of nutria

3 cups flour

Salt and pepper to taste

3 cups vegetable oil

Crack eggs into a bowl and stir in milk, seasonings, mustard, Worcestershire sauce, and hot sauce. Whisk well until batter is blended. Add nutria to the batter and soak for 2 hours before frying.

Mix flour with a little salt and pepper. Heat oil in a skillet to 350–375 degrees. Coat nutria in the flour mixture, shake off any excess, and place in oil to fry. Fry for about 5 minutes, until one side is golden brown, and then flip and repeat. Place the legs on paper towels to drain. You can serve them with Cajun dip or rice and beans.

NUTRIA PATTIES

SERVES 8 TO 10

2 pounds of deboned nutria

1 medium white potato, diced

$1/2$ cup sweet potatoes, minced

1 large onion, diced

1 large red bell pepper, diced

1 teaspoon garlic, minced

1 tablespoon parsley flakes

1 tablespoon Worcestershire sauce

$1/4$ cup green onions

2 large eggs

$1/2$ cup Italian bread crumbs

1 teaspoon mustard

2 tablespoons Gatorqueen's Bayou Seasoning

1 teaspoon D.a.T sauce

$1/4$ teaspoon salt

1 pinch black pepper

2 cups oil

Mince nutria in a food processor, and then place in a bowl. Mince potato, sweet potato, diced onions, diced bell pepper, and garlic in the food processor. Then add mixture to the meat and combine. Next add parsley flakes, Worcestershire sauce, green onions, eggs, bread crumbs, mustard, Bayou Seasoning, D.a.T sauce, salt, and pepper to your meat. Combine thoroughly until evenly mixed.

Heat oil in a large saucepan on medium heat until hot. Wet your hands slightly each time you form a patty, and then place them to fry. Fry patties until dark brown on one side, and then flip and repeat. Drain on paper towels and then they are ready to serve!

Recommended as a sandwich with lettuce, tomatoes, mayonnaise, mustard and ketchup.

FRIED RABBIT

SERVES 4

During hunting season in south Louisiana, the bag limit is 8 wild rabbits a day per person. Rabbits multiply fast down here in the marsh, and are lean and delicious.

1 rabbit, cut into pieces

1 cup half–and–half

1 teaspoon hot sauce

2 tablespoons mustard

3 large eggs

1 tablespoon parsley flakes

1/4 teaspoon red pepper

2 cups flour

Salt and pepper to taste

2 cups vegetable oil

In a medium bowl, place rabbit, half-and-half, hot sauce, mustard, eggs, parsley flakes, and red pepper. Mix this well until the batter is thoroughly combined with the rabbit. Marinate for 2 hours before frying.

Mix flour and a pinch of salt and pepper in a second bowl. Heat oil in a skillet. Pass the rabbit pieces from the batter to the flour mixture and put to fry. Flip occasionally and fry until golden brown on each side. Cook until tender.

Served best with potato salad and Cajun dip.

SMOTHERED RABBIT

SERVES 4

1 stick butter

1 large onion, diced

1 large bell pepper, diced

1 tablespoon garlic, minced

1 medium rabbit, cut up

1 teaspoon parsley flakes

1 teaspoon hot sauce

$1/2$ teaspoon red pepper

Salt and pepper to taste

1 (10-ounce) can cream of celery soup

3 cups water

1 cup cooked rice

In a large saucepan, melt butter and add onions, peppers, and garlic. Wilt this down, letting the onion mixture stick before stirring, for a brown color. In a large bowl, mix rabbit, parsley flakes, hot sauce, red pepper, and salt and pepper to your taste. Mix well, and then add this to the onions. Brown this mixture well, and then add cream of celery and water. Cook for 1 hour and 30 minutes, or until rabbit is tender. Should be very thick and full of gravy.

Best served over rice and with a green bean casserole.

RABBIT STEW

SERVES 8 TO 19

1 cup flour

1 1/4 cup vegetable oil, divided

2 large rabbits, cut into pieces

1/4 teaspoon salt, plus more

1/4 teaspoon pepper, plus more

1 large onion, diced

1 large red bell pepper, diced

1 tablespoon minced garlic

1 (10-ounce) can of Mild Rotel Diced Tomatoes and Green Chilies

1/2 cup ketchup

1 teaspoon hot sauce

1 tablespoon Worcestershire sauce

1/4 teaspoon red pepper

4 cups water

2 cups cooked rice

In a large pot, make your roux by combining the flour and 1 cup of the oil.

Place the rabbit into a bowl. Add 2 good-sized pinches of salt and pepper and mix well. Pour 1/4 cup oil into a skillet and brown the meat on both sides. Once it is browned, place back into the bowl.

Add onions, peppers, garlic and Rotel to your roux. Wilt this down for about 5 minutes. Add ketchup, hot sauce, Worcestershire sauce, 1/4 teaspoon of each salt and pepper, red pepper, and water. This should be stirred constantly to break up the roux. Then add the rabbit and cook for 2 hours. You may need to add more water if the meat is not tender enough or if the gravy thickens too quickly.

Served over cooked rice with white beans on the side.

SMOTHERED SQUIRREL

SERVES 4 TO 6

During hunting season in South Louisiana, there is a season on squirrels. They reproduce at a high rate and are very good to eat.

2 medium onions, diced

1 large bell pepper, diced

1 tablespoon minced garlic

$1/2$ cup sliced green onions

1 stick of butter

3 medium squirrels, cut into pieces

2 tablespoons Gatorqueen's Bayou Seasoning

$1/4$ teaspoon salt

1 tablespoon Worcestershire sauce

4 cups water

2 cups cooked rice

Place onions, peppers, garlic, green onions, and butter in a large pot. Wilt this down for about 15 minutes. In a medium-sized bowl, mix squirrel meat, Bayou Seasoning, salt, and Worcestershire sauce, and add to onion mixture. Stir well to brown your meat, and then add the water. Taste as you go; you may need to add more seasoning. Cook this down for 2 hours, until water is absorbed and gravy is thick.

Serve over rice with a green salad and white beans.

SQUIRREL SAUCE PIQUANT

SERVES 8 TO 10

4 tablespoons vegetable oil

4 tablespoons flour

2 large onions, diced

1 large bell pepper, diced

2 ribs of celery, diced

1 tablespoon minced garlic

1 (8-ounce) can of tomato paste

1 (10-ounce) can Mild Rotel Tomatoes and Green Chilies

1 (8-ounce) can of mushrooms

$^{1}/_{2}$ cup cut-up green onions

1 teaspoon parsley flakes

1 teaspoon allspice

Red pepper to taste

Salt and pepper to taste

6 squirrels, cut up

3 cups water

1 (10-ounce) can tomato sauce

1 teaspoon sugar

3 cups cooked rice

In a large oval pot, cook oil and flour over a low heat to make a peanut butter-colored roux. Add onions, peppers, celery, garlic, tomato paste, Rotel, and mushrooms. Sauté this into your roux on low heat. Then add green onions, parsley flakes, allspice, red pepper, and salt and pepper. Add squirrel meat and brown for a while, then add water while stirring constantly. Add tomato sauce and sugar. Cook this on medium heat for $1^{1}/_{2}$ to 2 hours.

Serve over rice, with white beans and smothered potatoes on the side.

SMOTHERED TURTLE

SERVES 6 TO 8

1 1/2 sticks of butter

2 medium onions, diced

1 large bell pepper, diced

1 tablespoon minced garlic

1 rib celery, chopped fine

5 pounds of cut-up turtle

1 tablespoon parsley flakes

1 (10-ounce) can cream of mushroom soup

2 tablespoons Gatorqueen's Bayou Seasoning

1/4 teaspoon salt

2 teaspoons Worcestershire sauce

1 teaspoon mustard

1 teaspoon ketchup

4 cups water

2 cups cooked rice

Place the butter in a large pot to melt; add the onions, peppers, garlic, and celery and wilt. Once the onions are softened, add your turtle and brown with the onions. Add parsley flakes, cream of mushroom, Bayou Seasoning, salt, Worcestershire sauce, mustard, ketchup, and water. Cook this down on medium heat for 2 hours. More time may be needed if the meat is not tender. The turtle should be falling off of the bone and have a thick gravy. Serve over rice.

Don't forget to suck the bucks! The flavor is amazing! Serve with baked beans and potato salad.

TURTLE FRICASSEE

SERVES 6 TO 8

1 cup flour

1 cup oil

5 pounds of cut-up snapping turtle

2 large onions, chopped

1 large bell pepper, chopped

2 tablespoons minced garlic

2 stalks celery, chopped finely

1 (10-ounce) can Mild Rotel Diced
Tomatoes and Green Chilies

$1/2$ cup finely chopped green onion tops

4 cups water

2 teaspoons Worcestershire sauce

1 teaspoon salt

$1/2$ teaspoon pepper

$1/4$ teaspoon cayenne pepper

2 cups cooked rice

In a skillet, cook flour and oil, stirring constantly, to make a peanut butter-colored roux. Add your turtle directly to the roux, stirring to brown the meat. Then add onions, peppers, garlic, celery, Rotel, and green onions, stirring really well. Then add the water, stirring constantly with a large cooking spoon to break up the roux. Add Worcestershire sauce, salt, pepper, and cayenne pepper. Taste the stew; you might have to add a little more seasoning. Cook on medium heat for 2 hours, until meat is tender.

Serve over cooked rice with potato salad and little sweet peas.

SIDES

POTATO SALAD

SERVES 8 TO 10

4 large white potatoes, peeled and cut into chunks

10 large eggs

1 cup real mayonnaise

1 1/2 tablespoons prepared mustard

1/2 teaspoon salt

1/4 teaspoon black pepper

1 pinch paprika

First place the potato chunks and eggs into a large pot and cover with water about 2 inches above potatoes. Bring to a boil and cook for about 15 minutes, or until potatoes are fork tender. Pour the cooked potatoes and eggs into a strainer, remove the eggs, and place potatoes back into the dry pot.

Peel the eggs and add them to the pot with the potatoes. Using a potato masher, smash the eggs and potatoes together until mixed well and not lumpy. Add the mayonnaise, mustard, salt and pepper, and mix until creamy. Sprinkle paprika over the top of your salad and serve.

CREAMED POTATOES

SERVES 5 TO 7

This is a really easy recipe that goes great as a side to many other main dishes, but also works as a meal of its own.

4 large white baking potatoes

3 cups water

1 (10-ounce) can evaporated milk

1 stick butter

1 teaspoon salt

$1/2$ teaspoon black pepper, or pepper of choice

Peel the potatoes and cut them in half lengthwise, then cut them into small slices about $1/4$ inch thick. Place the potatoes and water in a medium pot over high heat with the lid on. Bring to a boil and let cook about 10–12 minutes, or until fork tender. Strain off the water and place potatoes into a large bowl with the milk, butter, salt and pepper. Beat with a hand mixer until smooth.

I like mine served with hamburger steak.

GREEN BEAN CASSEROLE

SERVES 6 TO 8

$^1/_2$ stick of butter

1 medium onion, diced

$^1/_2$ cup chopped bell peppers

2 medium potatoes, diced

4 (14 ounce) cans French Style Green Beans

Salt and pepper to taste

8 slices American cheese

In a medium pot melt the butter. Add onions and peppers and cook until wilted. Add potatoes and stir well. Let the potatoes brown somewhat. Open the cans of green beans and drain the water. Pour the beans over the mixture and mix well. Add two good-sized pinches of salt and pepper. Add water just to cover the beans. Cook this down until all of the water is absorbed. Turn down to low heat and place slices of cheese all over the top of the green beans. Let the cheese melt, and then stir thoroughly.

The end result will be creamy and delicious!

CAJUN DIP

MAKES 1¼ CUPS

This dip goes well with just about anything, from most breakfast foods, to fried foods, and any kind of boiled seafood. It is very easy to make and has a unique flavor that will impress any company you may have over for a meal.

1 cup real mayonnaise

4 tablespoons ketchup

$^1/_2$ teaspoon hot sauce

1$^1/_2$ teaspoons Gatorqueen's Bayou Seasoning

$^1/_2$ teaspoon prepared mustard

$^1/_4$ teaspoon lemon juice

$^1/_2$ teaspoon garlic powder

In a small or medium bowl, mix all of the ingredients until well combined. Serve with fried or boiled foods, or as a spread in sandwiches.

STUFFED POTATO

SERVES 6

3 large baking potatoes

$^1/_2$ cup butter

$^1/_2$ cup sour cream

$^1/_2$ cup evaporated milk

1 pinch salt

1 pinch black pepper

1 pinch Gator Queen's Bayou Seasoning

1 (8-ounce) bag shredded mild cheddar cheese

Put the potatoes in the sink and run hot water over them. Poke holes in them with a knife on both sides. Next, place the potatoes on a plate, cover with moist paper towels and microwave for about 20 minutes on one side, then flip and cook for 20 minutes on the other side, or until done. Once the potatoes are tender, remove them from the microwave, hold them with a dry cloth and slice them in half. Spoon out hot potato into a bowl, and keep the shells on the side.

Add butter, sour cream, milk, salt, pepper, Bayou seasoning and half of the bag of cheese to potatoes. Stir until all is melted and blended together. Your mixture should be creamy. Next, get a spoon and fill the potato skins with the filling. Place the potatoes on a baking sheet and sprinkle remaining cheese on top. Bake at 350 degrees until the cheese is melted.

TARTAR SAUCE

MAKES ABOUT 4½ CUPS

This recipe is excellent to make when you have a lot of company over. Recommended with fried fish, shrimp, or crawfish.

1 (30-ounce) jar of mayonnaise

1 teaspoon lemon juice

½ teaspoon of Worcestershire sauce

1 small onion, minced well

½ cup dill pickles, minced

1 dab mustard

1 pinch Gator Queen's Bayou Seasoning

1 pinch salt

¼ teaspoon hot sauce

In a medium bowl, add the mayonnaise, lemon juice, Worcestershire sauce, onion, pickle, mustard, Bayou seasoning, salt, and hot sauce. Mix together thoroughly. Store in the refrigerator until ready to use.

BOUDIN DIP

MAKES AN 8 X 6 X 2-INCH PAN

4 links Boudin sausage

1 (8-ounce) package cream cheese

1 (8-ounce) container sour cream

2 tablespoons mayonnaise

1 (8-ounce) bag shredded cheddar cheese

1 pinch black pepper

1 pinch Gator Queen's Bayou Seasoning

Remove the Boudin from casing and cook in microwave for 3 minutes. Then place it in a bowl. Soften the cream cheese and add it to the Boudin along with the sour cream. Mix in all of the other ingredients. Place into a small pan and cook in the oven at 350 degrees for 10 minutes. Let it cool, and then it's ready to serve with crackers or on a slice of bread.

MAMA ELLA'S WHITE BEANS

SERVES 8 TO 10

For this recipe, your beans must soak in water for a while. If you are cooking them for lunch, you will need to begin soaking them the night before. If you are cooking them for a late supper, then you can begin soaking them early in the morning. This recipe goes great with just about any fried foods, over rice, or as a side for any rice and gravy.

4 pounds dried white navy beans, picked through

4 quarts water

1 large onion, diced

2 tablespoons minced garlic

1 cup finely diced green onions

1 cup Morrell Snow Cap Lard

1 teaspoon black pepper

1 1/2 teaspoons salt

Place the beans into a large pot and cover completely with water by about 3 inches; let them soak for about 8 hours or overnight.

Once you are ready to cook them, drain the beans and discard the soak water; rinse them thoroughly. Place the beans back into the pot and add 4 quarts of water along with the onions, garlic, green onions, lard, and seasonings. Cook uncovered over low-to-medium heat for about 2 hours, stirring occasionally. Before the beans are completely done, remove 2 cups of beans, smash them well, and then place them back into the pot and mix in. Cook for 10 more minutes over low heat.

MAMA ELLA'S RED BEANS

SERVES 6 TO 8

2 pounds red kidney beans

1 large onion, diced

1 large bell pepper, diced

2 tablespoons minced garlic

1 tablespoon parsley flakes

1 cup green onions, sliced

1/2 cup Morrell Snow Cap Lard

1 teaspoon black pepper

1 teaspoon salt

4 quarts water

Soak beans for at least 2 hours before cooking. After soaking, boil the beans for 25 minutes and strain. Add the beans to a pot along with all the other ingredients, and cook for 2 hours. When you start to see the beans breaking up, take a large cooking spoon and stir and smash the beans to the side of the pot until creamy.

Serve over rice or in a bowl with crackers.

BREAKFAST

SHRIMP OMELET

SERVES 4 TO 6

For this recipe be sure that you have American gulf shrimp. Imported shrimp will not have the same rich flavor and will definitely not be as fresh.

1 pound small Gulf shrimp, peeled

$1/2$ stick butter

1 large onion, diced

$1/2$ bell pepper, diced

2 tablespoons minced garlic

2 green onions, diced

1 teaspoon Gatorqueen's Bayou Seasoning

$1/4$ cup water

7 large eggs

$1/4$ cup whole milk

3 slices American cheese

Place shrimp into a bowl and set aside. In a medium skillet over medium heat, add the butter, onions, bell peppers, garlic, green onions, and Bayou seasoning. Cook for about 10–15 minutes, stirring often until onions are soft, wilted and golden brown. Add your shrimp and water to the skillet and cook down over medium heat, stirring often, until all the water has boiled out.

In a separate bowl, add the eggs and milk and scramble well. Once the water has cooked out of your skillet, add the scrambled eggs to the shrimp mixture and continue to cook over low-to-medium heat, stirring frequently, until the eggs are fully cooked. Finally add the slices of cheese over the top of the eggs to melt.

Serve with biscuits and hash brown potatoes.

SAUSAGE OMELET

SERVES 4

4 links pork sausage

12 large eggs

1 small onion, diced

1 medium bell pepper, diced

$1/4$ cup thinly sliced green onions

Pam Spray

1 (8 ounce) bag of shredded American or cheddar cheese

First, cut the sausage links into small pieces and place to the side. Crack the eggs into a bowl and whisk with onion, bell pepper, and green onion.

Spray a skillet with nonstick cooking spray and heat on low before pouring in the egg mixture. Let the eggs cook on the bottom, and then add sausage pieces. Flip half of the omelet over, letting both sides cook until brown. Move omelet to a plate with your spatula, add cheese on top, and then your omelet is ready to serve!

CRAWFISH OMELET

SERVES 3 TO 4

What better way to spice up your breakfast than with some Louisiana crawfish? Most of the time when we boil crawfish we have some left over, so we peel the remainder and use those tails for many other recipes. Nothing goes to waste. Be sure that your crawfish are not imported ones, because there is a big difference in taste.

1 pound crawfish tails, peeled
$^1/_2$ stick butter
1 onion, diced
$^1/_2$ bell pepper, diced
2 tablespoons minced garlic
2 green onions, diced

$1^1/_2$ teaspoons Gatorqueen's Bayou Seasoning
$^1/_2$ cup water
7 large eggs
$^1/_3$ cup whole milk
3 slices American cheese

To get started, have your crawfish ready in a bowl and set them to the side. In a medium skillet, melt the butter and add the onions, bell peppers, garlic, green onions, and Bayou Seasoning. Cook over medium heat, stirring often, until onions and peppers are wilted and golden brown, about 10–15 minutes. Add the crawfish to your skillet and continue to cook over medium heat, stirring often, for another 3 minutes. Add the water and let that cook on the same heat until it has boiled out.

In a separate bowl, add the eggs and milk and scramble together. Once the water has boiled out of your skillet, add the scrambled eggs to the crawfish mixture and continue to cook and stir until the eggs are cooked. Finally add the cheese over the top of the eggs and let it melt.

Goes great with fried potatoes.

FRIED BISCUITS

SERVES 4

This is a very easy and quick meal for your kids in the morning, or just a snack at night when you are craving something sweet.

1 container of 8 large refrigerator Buttermilk Biscuits
2 cups vegetable oil
Sugar for sprinkling
Aunt Jemima Original Lite Syrup

Pour vegetable oil into a skillet and place this to the side.

Open your biscuits and lay them flat on a cookie sheet to warm to room temperature. Poke holes in the biscuits with a fork and cut into fourths. Heat oil in a skillet and fry the biscuits on both sides. Keep a close eye on them, because they brown quickly. Drain on a paper towel. Set them on a plate and sprinkle sugar to your liking. Add syrup and then it's ready to eat! Yum!

FRIED BREAD DOUGH

SERVES 6 TO 8

This is a breakfast that my mom used to cook for my siblings and me all the time when we were growing up. I still cook it now for my kids and myself.

2 loaves frozen bread dough
2 cups vegetable oil
Sugar
Syrup

Place dough in a large bowl to rise overnight. Break the dough into small pieces and flatten out with your fingers.

Heat oil in a large skillet and put the bread pieces to fry in batches. Let them get golden brown on one side and then flip to the other side. Place on paper towels to drain. Add sugar and syrup as desired.

LIZ'S CAJUN BREAKFAST SANDWICH

SERVES 4 TO 6

1 loaf French bread

2 medium white potatoes

1 1/2 cups vegetable oil

1 dozen eggs

1 cup Cajun dip (page 147)

2 pounds turkey ham

2 large tomatoes, sliced thin

2 cups shredded lettuce

1 (8-ounce) package shredded American cheese

Take your loaf of bread and slice it lengthwise down the middle and place this to the side. Next, cut the potatoes into thin round slices and also place to the side.

Meanwhile, in a medium skillet, add the vegetable oil and heat over high heat until it is about 375 degrees. Add potato slices to the oil and cook until golden brown on both sides, then place in a separate dish on paper towels to absorb the oil; cover and place to the side.

Spray a separate skillet generously with nonstick cooking spray and heat over medium heat. Fry your eggs until the yolks are hard, remove from skillet to a plate, cover and set aside.

Preheat oven to 400 degrees.

Take the bottom half of your bread loaf and spread it with Cajun dip, then cover evenly with the potatoes, eggs, turkey ham, and tomato slices and lettuce. Top with the shredded cheese. Cover with the top portion of your bread loaf, place on a baking pan, and bake for about 10 minutes, until cheese is melted. Cut and serve.

LOST BREAD

SERVES 5

6 large eggs

1 (12 ounce) can of evaporated milk

$1/4$ cup of pure vanilla extract

1 tablespoon of sugar

1 pinch cinnamon

10 slices of bread

Spray a large skillet with nonstick cooking spray.

In a large bowl, crack the eggs and add milk, vanilla, sugar, and cinnamon. Mix well with a whisk. Soak bread in the mixture one slice at a time, keeping the bread moist.

When a couple pieces of bread are battered, heat skillet on medium heat. Place battered bread on your skillet to cook. Bread should be a golden brown color on each side. Repeat process until all pieces of bread are done.

Serve with powdered sugar on top or with syrup.

DESSERTS

MAMA ELLA'S CRACKER PUDDING

SERVES 10 TO 12

PUDDING

4 (12-ounce) cans evaporated milk

4 (12-ounce) cans water

8 egg yolks

$2^1/_2$ cups sugar

2 tablespoons vanilla extract

6 sleeves unsalted crackers

MERINGUE

4 tablespoons sugar

8 egg whites

Pour evaporated milk into a 18 x 12 x 3-inch pan. Into the same pan pour 4 cans of water. Crack and separate the eggs, putting the yolks in the milk and the whites in a separate bowl. Add $2^1/_2$ cups of sugar and vanilla extract to the pan, then whisk very well to incorporate. Next smash all the crackers in their sleeves, then pour the crackers into the milk mixture, stirring in well. Set aside.

In a blender, incorporate 4 tablespoons of sugar slowly into the egg whites. Blend until meringue is very thick and then pour over the crackers. Bake at 350 degrees F. for 35 minutes, until top gets golden brown. Then it's done. But it's even better when refrigerated; this way it will thicken and become a pudding. Let it cool completely before refrigerating.

BROWNIES

MAKES A 9 X 13-INCH PAN

4 teaspoons cocoa

$3/4$ cup vegetable oil

2 cups sugar

2 teaspoons vanilla extract

$1/4$ teaspoon salt

3 large eggs, beaten

1 cup all-purpose flour

1 teaspoon black walnut–flavored extract

1 can milk chocolate frosting

Preheat oven to 350 degrees. Prepare a 9 x 13-inch pan with nonstick cooking spray.

In a large bowl, mix all of the ingredients together except for the chocolate frosting Blend well.

Add the entire contents of the bowl to a 9 x 13-inch baking pan and level out the batter. Bake for 30 minutes. Remove from oven and let cool completely before spreading the chocolate frosting over the top. Let set for at least 30 minutes before digging in!

FAVORITE CHOCOLATE BALLS

MAKES 20 TO 25 BALLS

1 box devil's food cake mix

1 can German Chocolate frosting

1 (4-ounce) bar Baker's semisweet chocolate

Bake the cake according to package directions and allow it to cool to room temperature. Once cooled, smash or crush the entire cake into crumbs and place in a large bowl. Add the entire can of frosting, and mix it well with the cake crumbs. The more you mix it the moister the chocolate balls will be. When completely mixed, begin rolling them into golf ball–size balls.

In a separate pot, melt down the Baker's chocolate. Roll each ball in the melted chocolate and place on a cookie sheet or pan that has been covered with wax paper. Once they are cool and hard, they are ready to eat.

My mother-in-law, Gwendolyn Choate Hutchinson, contributed some of the dessert recipes. She made the cobblers on pages 181 and 182.

BANANA AND CHOCOLATE CAKE

SERVES 8

2 boxes banana cream instant pudding

1 box yellow cake mix

6 bananas, sliced into small pieces

1 can milk chocolate frosting

Prepare three 8-inch round cake pans with nonstick cooking spray.

Mix one box of pudding according to package directions. Next, mix the yellow cake mix in a large bowl according to package directions. Add the mixed pudding into the mixed cake batter and stir thoroughly together. Divide batter among the three cake pans Bake, following the directions on cake packaging. Once you have baked three layers of cake, let them cool down.

Mix the second pudding box in a bowl, and add banana slices. Mix evenly and then refrigerate for 15 minutes. When the cake layers are completely cooled, remove from pans and spread half of the pudding and banana mixture on the top of one layer of cake. Place another layer on top, and spread the other half of the banana mixture on top. Place the last layer on top and frost only the top layer of the cake with the milk chocolate frosting. Add sliced bananas on top of cake. Ready to serve!

SYRUP CAKE WITH JELLY TOPPING

SERVES 8 TO 10

1 cup water

1 cup sugar

$^1/_4$ teaspoon allspice

1 teaspoon cinnamon

$^1/_4$ teaspoon nutmeg

2 cups all-purpose flour

1 cup vegetable oil

1 cup dark syrup (Steen's or Blackburn)

3 large eggs, beaten

2 teaspoons baking soda

5 tablespoons grape jelly (or whatever flavor you prefer)

Preheat oven to 350 degrees. Prepare a 9 x 13-inch baking pan with nonstick cooking spray.

In a medium pot, add the water and bring to a boil. Remove from heat and add remaining ingredients in order listed, except the jelly, adding baking soda last. Mix well until baking soda is dissolved. Add batter to baking pan and mix well again. Bake for 40 minutes. Remove from oven and let the cake cool before spreading the jelly over the top of the cake.

HONEY BUN CAKE

SERVES 8

1 box yellow cake mix

3 large eggs, beaten

$3/4$ cup sugar

8 ounces sour cream

$1/4$ cup vegetable oil

$3/4$ cup brown sugar

4 tablespoons cinnamon

$1/2$ cup chopped pecans

1 cup powdered sugar

1 tablespoon whole milk

1 teaspoon vanilla extract

Preheat oven to 350 degrees. Prepare a 9 x 13-inch baking pan with nonstick cooking spray.

In a large bowl, add the cake mix, eggs, sugar, sour cream, and vegetable oil; mix together well. Pour cake batter into prepared baking pan and set aside.

In a small bowl, add the brown sugar, cinnamon, and pecans and mix together well. Add this mixture to the cake batter and swirl it around. Bake for 30–35 minutes, until cake is done.

Meanwhile, in another small bowl, add the powdered sugar, milk, and vanilla and mix well to make your glaze. Spread the glaze over the warm cake and serve.

DOUGHNUTS

MAKE 15 TO 20 DONUTS

1 tablespoon Crisco All-Vegetable Shortening

2 cups sugar

3 large eggs, beaten

2 cups evaporated milk

5 cups all-purpose flour

4 teaspoons baking powder

1 teaspoon nutmeg

1 teaspoon salt

2 cups vegetable oil

1 cup powdered sugar

In a large bowl, mix the shortening, sugar, eggs, milk, flour, baking powder, nutmeg, and salt together thoroughly. On the counter, knead the dough together lightly over and over until it is flattened and about 1/2 inch thick. Use a doughnut cutter, to cut out the doughnuts, and set them aside until you are ready to fry them.

Add the vegetable oil to a large skillet and heat to 375 degrees. Once oil is hot enough, add the pieces of dough a few at a time and fry until golden brown. Set them on paper towels to absorb excess oil and then roll them in the powdered sugar.

PEACH COBBLER

SERVES 5 TO 7

4 cups freshly sliced peaches

1^1/$_2$ cups sugar

1 teaspoon cornstarch

1^1/$_2$ cups self-rising flour or pancake mix

1 teaspoon cinnamon

1 stick butter, cut into cubes

1^1/$_2$ cups cold whole milk

Preheat oven to 350 degrees. Spray a 9 x 13-inch pan with nonstick cooking spray.

Mix peaches, sugar and cornstarch together and then place to the side.

Mix together flour, cinnamon, half of the butter cubes, and milk until the consistency is thicker than pancake batter.

Pour the peaches into the pan, and dot the remaining butter on top. Pour flour mixture over the top of peaches, and sprinkle with sugar and cinnamon. Bake for 1 hour, or until the top of the cobbler is golden brown.

BLACKBERRY COBBLER

SERVES 8 TO 10 PEOPLE

1 quart fresh blackberries

5 cups sugar, divided

1 tablespoon cornstarch

4 teaspoons baking powder

2 teaspoons vanilla extract

3 large eggs, beaten

1 1/2 cups Crisco Butter Flavor All-Vegetable Shortening

1/4 teaspoon salt

1 cup evaporated milk

6 cups all-purpose flour

Preheat oven to 350 degrees. Prepare a deep baking pan about 18 x 12 x 3 inches with nonstick cooking spray.

In a medium pot add your blackberries and 1 cup of sugar; mix well. Cook over medium heat for 20 minutes, stirring often. Add the cornstarch and stir in well to thicken the berry mixture. Remove from heat and set aside.

In a large bowl, mix together the baking powder, 4 cups sugar, vanilla extract, eggs, Crisco and salt. Then add the milk and flour last. Mix all of these ingredients well, making a thick dough. Roll out the dough to about 1/2 inch thick and lay it over the top of your berries. Bake for about 25 minutes, or until the top of the dough is golden brown. Great served hot or cold.

7-UP CAKE

SERVES 8

1 box yellow cake mix

8 ounces 7-UP

2 (8-ounce) boxes pineapple cream or
banana cream instant pudding

6 large eggs, divided

2 cups sugar

4 tablespoons all-purpose flour

1 stick butter

1 (16-ounce) can crushed pineapple

Preheat oven to 350 degrees. Prepare three 8-inch round cake pans with nonstick cooking spray.

In a large bowl, add the cake mix, 7-UP, instant pudding, and 4 beaten eggs and mix well. Divide the batter into 3 small cake pans and bake for 35–40 minutes. Once cooked, remove from oven and set aside to cool. When cool, remove cakes from pans.

To make the topping, in a large bowl mix together the sugar and flour well. Add remaining 2 eggs, butter, and crushed pineapple and mix thoroughly. Place this mixture into a small pot over low heat and cook until thick, stirring constantly to make sure eggs blend in. Let the topping cool.

Spread the topping over each of the three cake layers and stack one on top of the next until you have a 3-layer cake. Spread topping around the sides and you are ready to serve.

INDEX

PHOTO CREDITS

METRIC CONVERSION CHART

Volume Measurements		Weight Measurements		Temperature Conversion	
U.S.	Metric	U.S.	Metric	Fahrenheit	Celsius
1 teaspoon	5 ml	$1/2$ ounce	15 g	250	120
1 tablespoon	15 ml	1 ounce	30 g	300	150
$1/4$ cup	60 ml	3 ounces	90 g	325	160
$1/3$ cup	75 ml	4 ounces	115 g	350	180
$1/2$ cup	125 ml	8 ounces	225 g	375	190
$2/3$ cup	150 ml	12 ounces	350 g	400	200
$3/4$ cup	175 ml	1 pound	450 g	425	220
1 cup	250 ml	$2 1/4$ pounds	1 kg	450	230